The Black-and-White

Thinking Christian

Moving Beyond the
All or Nothing Mindset
to Become Like Christ

Fred Jacoby, MA

The Black-and-White Thinking Christian

Copyright © 2019 by Fred Jacoby

Editor: Judy Hagey www.judyhagey.com

Photo: Peter Kaedy www.pk3photography.com

ISBN - 978-1-7340312-0-1

To Contact the Author:

www.fredjacoby.com

www.foundchristcounsel.org

www.facebook.com/fredkjacoby

Table of Contents

Preface

In my role as Executive Director of Foundations Christian Counseling Services, I've had the privilege of blogging about many topics, including marriage, communication, grace, and basic Christian living. The one series I enjoyed working through the most is the Black-and-White Thinking series. In fact, this series is the most read of those I have written. As I searched God's Word through this series, I gained additional insight into how we are created in the image of God and how black-and-white thinking reflects Him.

Most theologians agree that being created in His image involves our emotions, purpose, intelligence, and abilities—all which reflect God in many ways. In the Old Testament and in Revelation, God presents Himself as being black and white. God is not all black and white, of course; He is also relational, as emphasized through Christ in the New Testament. Understanding this led me to conclude the following: Not only does our creation as image bearers reflect our emotions, purpose, intelligence, and abilities, but also includes how we process and interpret, well, everything. Our interpretive lens is a direct reflection of God, our Father and Creator, and black-and-white thinking is one of the interpretive lenses people possess.

The Black-and-White Thinking series began a process of understanding which later developed into the Image Model. The Image Model is a Christ-centered framework for understanding God's image in us. More specifically, in understanding our interpretive lens, we understand ourselves and others better. In this model, those who possess black-and-white thinking are referred to as Moral Operators, while those who interpret things more relationally are considered Relational Operators. As we begin to understand ourselves better and clarify where we fall short, we will also be able to develop a path, through His Word and with His Spirit, to become like Christ, who is the "image of the invisible God."

While I don't discuss the Image Model in this book, you are invited to go to *www.fredjacoby.com* to explore this concept further. Soon, this book, tentatively titled *By Design: Created Like Him. Relating Like Him. Becoming Like Him*, will be available for purchase.

The *Black-and-White Thinking Christian* began with a series of blogs later edited with multiple additions and examples to add clarity and depth. It is my journey of understanding that led to the Image Model. While more could be written in every section, I will leave this for the future book. Until then, I hope you enjoy this overview of *The Black-and-White Thinking Christian*.

Disclaimer: The examples of couples and situations in this book are adapted from real life examples, whether from the counseling room or personal knowledge of circumstances in churches or others' lives. Of course, names in the narratives have been changed and details have been changed or omitted to protect the confidentiality of the couples. While these situations reflect reality, I am hopeful that readers will learn from these interactions, and grow in wisdom and love with our Savior and with others.

Acknowledgments

I want to thank my God for giving me insight into His Word regarding black-and-white thinking. Without Him, this endeavor is useless and purposeless. May He receive the glory for this work.

Thank you to my wife, who has been my greatest supporter throughout the years. Andrea, you are my best friend, encourager, and love of my life.

Of course, thank you to my family and friends who have also been a constant support and encouragement in my life. Thank you to my beta team who read this and offered suggestions and improvements.

Thank you to my editor, Judy, for your gracious efforts to turn this work into something the readers can better understand.

Finally, thank you, reader, for your trust in acquiring this resource for your personal and spiritual growth. I hope God will use this to help you grow in your walk with Christ and within your relationships.

1

Black-and-White vs. Relational Thinking

Thinking back over my counseling experiences, I noticed a certain population with whom I've had a difficult time connecting. It's not that the counsel was inadequate, per se, but that the counsel was not connecting with how they operate. As I considered these clients and the similarities among them, I concluded that they tend to be black-and-white thinkers.

In this book, I explore black-and-white thinkers from a biblical point of view, taking into account how we are created in His image and how we can grow in faith and relationships. But first things first, what are black-and-white thinkers and how are they different from relational thinkers?

Black-and-white thinkers are typically described as believing in all or nothing, good or bad, right or wrong, strong or weak, and smart or stupid. There is often no middle ground or gray area. Black-and-white thinkers typically focus on the tangible—things that can be seen, touched, heard or measured. They are often results-oriented, focusing on the process, procedures, and outcomes. The emotional processes, reasons and motives involved in decisions (the heart) are often irrelevant or difficult to grasp. In

1

other words, they focus on what is concrete rather than abstract. Black-and-white thinkers make decisions based on what is right or wrong in their perspective. They see actions as either-or. Either they love me and will show it in the way I desire, or they don't love me. Either the kids do what I say when I say it, or they are disobedient. Some more extreme black-and-white thinkers generally recognize their need for relationships, but they have a harder time connecting emotionally.

Further research, primarily from a secular viewpoint, considers such thinking mostly as a negative. Many articles call it a cognitive disorder, splitting, or dichotomous thinking. While black-and-white thinking is involved in mental health issues (see Chap 14), this book will mostly explore the everyday black-and-white thinking person who functions fairly well in society, yet may struggle in relationships. If you're not sure whether you are a black-and-white thinker or not, turn to Appendix A in the back of the book and take the quiz.

The term *relational thinkers* describes what is most important to another type of person—relationships. interpret circumstances and conversations through a relational lens, being more concerned with the impact on feelings, thoughts, and relationships. These folks live in the gray. Hardly anything is black-and-white. Relational thinkers tend to be more flexible in judging both actions and people for the sake of the relationship. Relational thinkers gravitate toward empathy—imagining themselves in the situation of another while experiencing similar emotions, and sympathy—showing compassion or sorrow for another going through a difficult time. They will focus more on the abstract, behind the scenes stuff, such as emotions, thoughts, motives, and desires, and are generally more considerate of other's feelings.

In an argument, relational thinkers tend to give in to others for the relationships' sake while black-and-white thinkers are apt to stand on what they see as absolute truths or facts. In other words, relational thinkers will focus on the *relationship* while the black-and-white thinkers will focus on the *content*. Each one concentrates on what is most important to them. This difference causes many frustrations in relationships.

We are not solely black-and-white thinkers or relational thinkers. It is not an either-or type of thinking. (It would be black-and-white for me to say so!) But the stronger our tendency toward black-and-white thinking, the more likely we are to live by the law—a rigid set of standards and expectations. The more relational we are, the more likely we make our decisions based on how we feel and what we think is best for relationships. Those who possess more black-and-white thinker qualities than relational thinker qualities are, for the purposes of this book, black-and-white thinkers.

As humans created in the image of God, I believe it is crucial to see how both types of thinkers can reflect Him. You see, God is both moral and relational. Absolute truth, as well as absolute right and wrong, exist because it is His universe. Throughout His Word, He explains what *wrong* is, i.e., sin. Yet, as His Word defines what is sinful, these wrongs are also explained in the greater context of the relationship between Him and us—His Bride, the church, and the bridegroom, Christ.

Author and speaker, Dr. Paul Tripp said, "Sin is not first about the breaking of an abstract set of rules. Sin is first and foremost about breaking relationship with God."[1] In declaring what is wrong, God seeks the greater good for us—to have a right relationship with Him that comes through faith and repenting of sin. The Old Testament establishes the rules or laws, yet they point to the New Testament where Christ's love and sacrifice paved the way for us lawbreakers to come to the Father. The presence of moral laws was not only necessary for humanity to know what is right and wrong, but to know a relational God as well.

Both types of thinkers are image bearers of God, yet, we ought to recognize that sin has stained the way we process, interpret, or perceive with in our hearts and minds.

Black-and-white thinkers ought to realize that when they interpret and perceive things as right and wrong, they often define right and wrong in their terms, not necessarily God's.

Glen was a devout follower of Christ. He attended First Baptist Church nearly every Sunday since childhood. Glen desired to honor God each Sunday with a suit and tie, which he thought every man should wear. To wear anything less than a tie, he thought, is dishonoring God. He even mentioned this to a number of younger parishioners who liked to wear polos or t-shirts. Glen had the freedom to wear a suit and tie to honor God, yet his definition of what is right and wrong may have been defined more by tradition than God's Word. His response to others also showed a lack of acceptance for others who didn't measure up to such standards. I believe God accepted Glen's actions of honoring Him through His attire as it demonstrated a heart's desire to honor. Yet looking down on others was an area that God would also desire to change.

Black-and-white thinkers might ask themselves these questions: Is my definition of what is right or wrong about my kingdom, tradition, or about God's kingdom? Am I becoming like a Pharisee focusing on how others need to behave while I'm blind to my own sins? How do I respond when others don't act right? When I speak the truth, do I do so in love?

Relational thinkers, with their tendency to see things relationally, may be so focused on having a good relationship that they refuse to deal with their own sin or overlook others' shortcomings. They might benefit from asking these questions: Am I so focused on love and feeling good that I make moral compromises? Am I sidestepping my children's discipline in order to have a good relationship with them? Am I trying to please people, yet not pleasing God? Do I skirt around issues to avoid hurting people's feelings, avoid difficult conversations and conflict, or avoid speaking the truth that may help them?

Neither relational thinkers nor black-and-white thinkers are more right or holy or better than the other. God, in His infinite wisdom, has created both, and He often places them together for the betterment of a family, ministry, or business. The strengths of the relational thinker will help with the weaknesses of the black-and-white thinker, and the strengths of the black-and-white thinker will complement the weaknesses of the relational thinker. When both recognize their strengths and weaknesses, and follow Christ's path of humility and grace, they can become an excellent team.

Reflection Questions:

1. According to others, what are your greatest assets in being a black-and-white or relational thinker?

2. If you are married, how does your partner's strengths complement your weaknesses?

3. How does your definition of right and wrong compare to God's definition of right and wrong? Even if they are the same, do your actions toward those who are in the wrong reflect the love of Christ in the Gospels, or more the judgment seat of Christ in Revelation?

2

Through a Biblical Lens

As believers in Jesus Christ, our main resource for truth and spiritual growth lies in the Word of God. Through His Word, we are able to interpret the world, discern what is of God and what is evil, grow in our relationship with God through Christ, and learn how to deny ourselves and love others. Paul states that God's Word is "useful for teaching, rebuking, correcting and training in righteousness" (2 Tim 3:16).

While black-and-white thinking is a modern term, many people from Adam to the present have had this type of thinking. Reading the accounts of Scripture, we may conclude prophets, kings, and disciples operated with black-and-white thinking. Joseph was likely a black-and-white thinker. His ability to organize and manage multiple tasks, develop processes and procedures including collecting and storing grain for a nation during a severe drought, would lead us to conclude he, at minimum, had black-and-white thinking tendencies. Even God presents himself as a black-and-white thinker throughout the Old Testament and the book of Revelation. He is all or nothing, desires us to be either hot or cold rather than lukewarm, establishes standards of living, judges according to these standards, and establishes processes and procedures for His followers. God, of course, not only possesses a black-and-white nature to Him, be He is also very relational as well. He pursues us in His love and grace, showing compassion and desiring to be close and intimate with us, His creation.

Many black-and-white thinkers see the world through the interpretive moral lens of right and wrong and measured standards. For example, judging others actions, appearance, or approaches based on what is ideal (how it should be) in their minds is very common. Additionally, black-and-white thinkers often have a stronger desire for tangible rewards and measured consequences for behaviors. Reading through the Scriptures, the group of people who possess these same qualities are the Pharisees. Jesus had more than a few things to say to the Pharisees throughout the Gospels. Let's take a look at one of them.

In Luke 15, Luke shares a parable of Jesus that attempts to reach the heart of the black-and-white thinking Pharisee. In the parable of the prodigal son, Jesus speaks of the younger son who did everything wrong. He essentially told his father he wished he were dead, took his inheritance before the father passed, was greedy, selfish, and lived his life for himself. Meanwhile, the older brother chose to honor his father by remaining with him and working for him. He did everything right. But when the younger brother returned, he became incensed when he saw his father's mercy and his brother's reinstatement into the family. The older brother refused to come to the party to celebrate his return.

The older brother mentality is the same as black-and-white thinking. It aligns with the Pharisees' thought processes. The older brother saw how the actions of the younger brother hurt his father, all while he did the good and right thing. In his eyes, the younger brother sinned by doing wrong, while he did not. He concluded that the younger brother did not deserve what a good person deserved. Naturally, the older brother considered himself the model of a "good person." The black-and-white thinker's abiding law is, "If you serve well, you deserve well. If you serve poorly, you deserve nothing." Tangible rewards and consequences are to be earned solely on merit, nothing more and nothing less. The merit system works well for bosses and employees in the workplace, but falls short in deeper, personal relationships.

The older brother needed to learn that even though there is right and wrong, the relationship with the offending party is just as significant as their actions. Actions alone do not dictate rewards and consequences, but rewards and consequences are directed by relationship, too. The older brother did not regard the relationship important when considering a reward or consequence. Anything given more or less than what was deserved, especially if compared to what he received (Lk 15:29), was seen as unfair.

In this parable, Jesus was addressing the Pharisees and implied that they were the older brother. The older brother, or the

Pharisees, failed to realize or acknowledge their self-righteous attitudes. The older son thought he was better than his younger brother because of his loyal and dedicated works. He failed to see, however, that he needed the father's mercy and grace as much as the younger brother.

Although we don't know if the younger brother was a relational thinker or a black-and-white thinker, his thought process echoed his brother's. Upon returning, he thought he should be treated like one of his father's servants. He thought he did not deserve anything more considering all he had done, yet he was most likely surprised by his father's loving, undeserved response. In acknowledging his unworthiness, the self-centered son repents of his sin and finds a welcome in the father's home.

At the end of the parable, the audience is left with an invitation from the father (God) to celebrate the restoration of a broken relationship (Lk 15:31–32). The older son was invited to recognize and celebrate the importance of a person who comes to repent and to put aside resentments, self-righteousness, and slander toward an undeserving person. Jesus was inviting his listeners to see their relationship with Him and others as one built not on actions and rewards, but on forgiveness, love, mercy, and grace. These are the essential ingredients of close relationships.

The black-and-white thinker typically has an older brother mentality. They will look at actions and rewards, and probably compare themselves and their actions to others. They may tend to see themselves as better than others and even more deserving. They may see things as fair or unfair and may even become angry when others get what they don't deserve or when they don't get what they think they deserve.

Jesus's message to the Pharisees in this passage is to recognize that the Father's response to sinners is not simply about actions and the law of works—you get what you deserve. No, Jesus wants them to recognize that when sinners repent from their ways, the Father is ready and willing to accept them and give them what they don't deserve—a full relationship with the Father that is not built upon works but upon His grace. Without grace, relationships often fail or at best, are shallow.

Throughout the Scriptures, we see the continuous themes of the law and grace. Some biblical characters may have more black-and-white tendencies, which tend to be more about law, while others may be more relational, which tends to favor grace. God, himself, shows both sides throughout the Old Testament and New Testament alike, demonstrating that both are not mutually exclusive of the other, but necessary for the other. Gleaning such truths from Scripture will guide us in understanding how we both reflect Him and can become more like Him. This is how we live life through a biblical lens.

Reflection Questions:

1. Black-and-white thinking reflects a characteristic of God that is black-and-white, and is seen mostly in the Old Testament and Revelation. What other areas do you see God as black-and-white? How is He relational?

2. If you were the older brother, would you celebrate your younger brother's return and a relationship restored? Would you join the party because you know that you should attend, but remain bitter inside? Or would you remain outside and complain that it is unfair and unjust? The Father's invitation is waiting your reply.

3

The Christian Walk

Whether in the counseling office, at church, or at home, all of us either know a person who thinks in black-and-white or we are one. Christians are as different from one another as are the rest of the world. Our personalities, appearances, interests, and tastes vary immensely. Yet our shared beliefs in Jesus Christ's life, death and resurrection and our trust in His Word unite us to live out our faith together. How we interpret Scripture, perceive events, and treat our fellow Christians will partly depend on whether our thinking is black-and-white or relational. Let's notice how the typical black-and-white thinker lives out their faith.

As noted previously, black-and-white thinkers often focus more on actions than motives or desires, although the heart is certainly acknowledged. Typically, in the heart of the black-and-white thinking Christian, the motives focus on the importance of obedience to the Word or law. If you are not obedient, which is right, you are disobedient, which is wrong. And if you are wrong, consequences are deserved. And essentially, this is correct thinking. The black-and-white thinking Christian emphasizes obedience yet may have more difficulty feeling or understanding the relational component that is also important in the Christian faith. While some acknowledge that Christianity is not about religion, but a relationship, the relationship is often lived out by works, which may lean toward religion.

A black-and-white thinker may verbalize their approach this way: "I'm a Christian. I believe all Jesus did for me. Now, just tell me what to do, and I will do it." Regular devotions and physical service, for example, are common demonstrations of love and commitment because they are concrete ways to show love and honor. Relational thinkers often need to focus more on God's love for them or compassion for others as motivation for doing something for Him. They may de-emphasize obedience to God, but their love and compassion may lead them to serve. Black-and-white thinking Christians, however, are more likely to focus on obedience to God and have difficulty with less concrete things, such as the feelings and emotions of faith, though some more passionate black-and-and-white thinkers may be led by their emotions. According to Jesus's words in John 14:15, 23, "If you love me, you will keep my commandments" or "obey me." This verse captures the love many black-and-white thinking Christians express toward God. It is a love demonstrated mostly through obedience.

One of the main concerns of black-and-white thinking Christians in the church and in family life is that grace becomes a license for people to sin (see Romans 6:1–2). This matter is one of the reasons grace is a difficult concept for many. If you extend grace—a relational concept—to others, they will take advantage. They won't learn, and they will be more disobedient. If fellow Christians live by grace, as opposed to obedience, they will not regularly act according to God's Word. Since obedience is such an important dimension of faith, grace seems to stand in contradiction to obedience. The black-and-white thinking Christian needs to comprehend that it is God's grace that empowers obedience—not our own will. A lack of grace will lead to legalism.

Overemphasizing either grace or obedience poses a danger to our faith. Too much emphasis on grace cheapens it. Paul states, "What shall we say, then? Shall we go on sinning so that grace may increase? By no means!" (Rom 6:1–2). Stressing obedience raises a concern about the standard to which we hold people. Adhering to a moral standard is certainly important in the life of a believer, but it is not the standard by which we are to determine whether we or others are good-real or bad-fake Christians. Christ's obedience on the cross is the measure of obedience by which we are considered righteous by faith.

One additional caution for black-and-white thinking Christians is to recognize that relationship is just as necessary as obedience. This relationship between God and us was made possible only through God's love and grace. "We love because God first loved us" (1 Jn 4:19). God's love was not made possible through our actions. We will never be able to earn God's favor or attention through our works. Therefore, all of us, relational thinkers and black-and-white thinking Christians alike, need to remember to focus specifically on Him and His love and grace through the cross and not on our own or other people's works. Our treatment of others must reflect our relationship with God through Christ, based on His grace and mercy to us, and not on others' obedience.

Finally, paying attention to the vertical relationship with God through Christ will help us acknowledge our blindness. Often, while focusing on obedience to certain standards, we can be blinded to the relational commands in Scripture. For example, we may speak truth to those who are disobedient, but we are often blind to the fact that in speaking truth, we do not speak it "in love" (Eph 4:15). When "speaking the truth" overshadows "in love," the spoken truth ceases to carry the weight of the entire truth. Without love, truth spoken often appears to be self-righteous judgment.

Drew was a devout Christian who knew God's Word better than the average Christian. He could teach classes or small groups at his church easily. During discussion times, he was asked questions about his teachings, and he was happy to respond. In a short time, people began to notice that his teachings involved a great deal of truth, which they appreciated, but his responses lacked a love for people. His hard line on obedience and truth lacked grace and appeared judgmental to many. While some in the church loved his classes and followed him, others decided not to

17

attend. Drew was aware that some no longer attended his courses, but dismissed them as immature Christians who were not dedicated to truth. Drew was leaning so much on speaking the truth, he ignored the love the Savior has for his people. As a result, Drew's class size dwindled.

While Drew may have struggled in teaching, he also served as an elder in his church. When situations arose about biblical interpretation and culture, he typically did not waver with the revealed Word. The pastor appreciated Drew's commitment to the gospel. While they disagreed with how to approach certain issues, Drew and his pastor respected each other enough to work well together.

Although it may seem black-and-white thinking is a detriment to the church, it is certainly not! Black-and-white thinking Christians are extremely important to the body of Christ. Although I've mentioned some weaknesses and cautions, let me share several significant strengths as well. The black-and-white thinking Christian's passion for standing for the truth and the Word of God is exemplary. Such a person often guides and challenges those around them—hopefully, in a good way. Though personal feelings may heavily influence the interpretation of Scripture in a relational person, feelings are typically submissive to the truth with Christian black-and-white thinkers. Any feelings a black-and-white thinker has are more a response to the truth (or of other people's not believing the truth). Without this anchor to the truth, the Christian faith can easily become watered down if we give in to the demands of the "feel good" culture or even the fears of our hearts. If we cannot stand with the truth, we will fall in step with the world.

Additionally, many black-and-white thinkers in the church are also the hands and feet—the doers within the church. They often organize events, structure meetings, dot the i's and cross the t's, oversee the finances and lead ministries efficiently. The attention to detail is absolutely necessary for excellence and accountability within the church or organization. Without black-and-white thinkers, churches and ministries would cease to function well and churches would fall apart.

They say the greatest strengths are also the greatest weaknesses. This can also be true. While I cover many areas of growth and offer a number of cautions, remember that black-and-white thinkers are created in God's image and complement relational thinkers, who have their own strengths and weaknesses. Together as the body of Christ, we can do much together.

Reflection Questions:

1. Do you struggle more with "speaking the truth" or speaking the truth "in love"? How?

2. Generally speaking, how do you show your love toward God? Is it expressed mostly in acts of service or by emotional praise? Or both? Explain.

3. What are your greatest strengths as a black-and-white thinker? How do you use these strengths for the church? How might these strengths also be weaknesses?

4

Grace and Works

Cindy is a black-and-white thinker. She's been married for ten years, but her world began to collapse when she discovered her husband, Kevin, had been having an emotional affair with a woman at work. In counseling, Kevin was able to share that his wife was a good woman, but he felt he could never do right in her eyes. He felt constantly criticized and unable to meet her expectations, opening a door of temptation for a woman at work who praised Kevin on a regular basis. Cindy never thought she criticized her husband, but digging deeper, she understood she had high standards for him. When he did not meet them, she would make comments to him in hopes he would change. These comments enforced Kevin's belief that she did not accept him as he was, but only if he became someone else.

Another way of looking at standards and expectations is to see them as laws. These laws, established in our hearts, dictate what a person should do, when they should do it, and how they should do it. In fact, anytime you hear or say the words "should" or "should not" is a telltale sign that you are measuring according to a standard or law. We may make laws for ourselves or for others.

Yet when these laws are not obeyed, often criticisms, comments, or consequences soon follow. This is what happened with Cindy and Kevin's marriage. While Kevin responded sinfully, Cindy's laws for Kevin played a role in creating an environment based on works. He felt like he had to do what she wanted to make her happy and avoid criticism.

The law of works, a theological concept mentioned in Scripture, is a common struggle for many black-and-white thinkers. This law states that one has to meet the standard, whether physical, moral, or relational, and then the person gets rewarded or receives consequences based on one's actions. As black-and-white thinkers are results-oriented and fruit-focused, many measure performance (works) and respond to the performance. Yet the other law mentioned in Scripture is the law of grace. This law is not about works, but about unearned favor.

Grace is a difficult truth for anyone to comprehend, let alone the black-and-white thinker. Grace is intangible. It cannot be seen or measured, though the effects are evident in a person's life. Grace remains elusive to many who have been enslaved to black-and-white thinking.

Having read Paul's letters in the New Testament, I believe him to be the most influential black-and-white thinker of the Bible. Paul, formerly known as Saul, was raised as a member of a strict Jewish sect known as the Pharisees. Saul was rising in the ranks of the Pharisees, even calling himself faultless based on the law

(Php 3:5–6, Acts 23:6). Before his conversion, Scripture portrayed Saul as zealous for the law, having been well-trained in the law and supported himself by meting out consequences for those who disobeyed the law. He even approved and possibly took part in the stoning of Stephen (Acts 7:58–8:1). We can infer that he was a black-and-white thinker with an added passion for justice as defined by the Pharisees.

While Saul was living by the law and persecuting the Christians, he had a life-changing experience on the road to Damascus. Miraculously, a relational Jesus confronted Saul. Jesus simply asked him, "Saul, why do you persecute me?" (Acts 9:4). This question had profound implications for Saul. Though the light blinded him, he began to see for the first time that what he thought was right, was actually wrong. In addition, his thinking and subsequent actions had personally impacted Jesus Christ. Saul's supernatural experience with Jesus changed him and the way he thought and acted.

After considering his horrible deeds, answering God's call to ministry, and receiving gospel training, Saul, now named Paul, became aware of a different law at work. He moved from living by the law of works to living by the law of grace. He wrote about grace frequently in his letters to the churches. Most of Paul's letters started with the following exhortation: "Grace and peace to you from God our Father and the Lord Jesus Christ." Paul wanted the people of God to know that "it is by grace you are saved, not by works" (Eph 2:8). In recognizing God's grace in his life, Paul moved from thinking primarily in black and white to thinking more relationally through grace. That is, our relationship with God is not one we earn, but one that occurs only by the grace and mercy of God through Christ.

Now, does this mean that Paul ceased all black-and-white thinking? I don't think so, but I do think his black-and-white thinking significantly decreased when he encountered God's grace. Paul still called for strict consequences for those who sinned, but he also was willing to show grace and mercy to those who asked for forgiveness (see 1 Cor 5:11–12, Titus 3:9–11, 2 Cor 2:5–11).

If you are a black-and-white thinker longing to grow in your faith and relationships with those around you, I strongly recommend growing in your understanding and application of grace. One fantastic resource on grace is the book *Transforming Grace* by Jerry Bridges. This resource illustrates how we set up laws in our hearts for ourselves and others and how we can instead live by grace. Don't simply read a book on grace and be done, but surround yourself with godly men or women who comprehend grace and can help you apply it to your life and relationships. Meeting Jesus and experiencing his grace transformed Saul. That encounter set him on a new course for his life and relationships with God and others. Understanding and applying grace will transform our lives too.

Reflection Questions:

1. What is your understanding of grace? Do you struggle with grace because people see it as a license to sin or for another reason?

2. What relationships in your life ought to be more filled with grace than judged by works? How will you show the undeserved favor you received from God to other people?

3. When do you most often say or think the words "should' or "should not"? Do you do this more often with others, or with yourself? Explain.

5

Differences Between Men and Women

Men are from Mars. Women are from Venus. Men are like waffles. Women are like spaghetti. Without a doubt, men and women are different, yet both can be black-and-white thinkers. Even though there are some similarities in black-and-white thinking between the sexes, there are some differences as well.

Similarities

To review, black-and-white thinking for both men and women involves processing events and situations as all or nothing, either-or, or right or wrong. Such thinking oversimplifies all the ins and outs of conditions and reduces them to two choices. Since there are only two choices—good or bad, right or wrong—it is important to meet the standard and achieve success, or else you fail and see yourself as bad. While standards can be good, setting standards without a measure of grace is unwise. Black-and-white thinking may lead to setting high standards for others and criticizing them when they fail to meet them. Such interactions will cause those close to you to feel insecure, lonely, and resentful. In abusive situations, black-and-white thinking is combined with pride, insecurity, and anger, which leads to controlling behaviors. Standards set for others are often both relational laws and activity laws. Relational laws are often created out of insecurity in order to feel loved or respected. Activity laws are standards set where the other person must meet a measured quantity or quality, sometimes within a specific timeframe. A spouse must complete the honey-do list around the house and shouldn't rest or watch TV until finished. A roommate doesn't clean well enough and leaves spots on the counter and soap scum in the shower. A child does not clean their room well enough before bedtime. Such standards are not inherently bad, but will depend on one's reaction when the expectation is not met. If resentments or attacks occur, relationships will be damaged.

Differences

Generally, men and women who think or process things in black-and-white do so differently because they are created and experience the world differently. Societal norms, hormones, past events and previous relationships will certainly influence how one perceives, processes, and acts. These influences will also impact the degree of black-and-white thinking that is present in the individual. Typically, the greater the hurts, the more broken the relationships or more traumatic the past, the greater propensity toward black-and-white thinking. In all cases, when black-and-white thinking merges with pride, the individual insists they are right and demands to have their way in the relationship (see chapter 7). A person who believes they are right cannot admit to being wrong. This leads to blame-shifting, minimizing one's own behaviors, dismissing the impact of one's behaviors, and strong reactions against others. It is important to be mindful of these norms as they can harm the relationship causing hurt feelings, fears, and resentments. The greatest differences between men and women who are black-and-white thinkers arise from the creation account, the reasons for our creation, and the desires of each. Let's briefly take a look at each.

Ladies First

In general, women seem to be more relational and probably less black-and-white in their thinking than men. I believe God created women to be relational. This conclusion is based on their anatomy which equips them to give birth and breastfeed thus forming a unique bond with their children. In addition, the order in which God created and the reasons for forming the first woman suggest that the focus for which God created woman was *for* relationship with man (Gen 3, 1 Cor 11:9). "It was not good for man to be alone. I will make a helper suitable for him" (Gen 2:18). It makes sense that women are generally more relational and less black-and-white in their thinking, or at least, the content of their black-and-white thinking may be more relationship oriented. For example, in many female black-and-white thinkers with whom I have spoken, their black-and-white thinking often occurs as relational laws. Your husband *must* love you by spending time together, serving, and performing similar acts that demonstrate love. When there's a right way to love, the relationship suffers. A husband must meet the standard or face punishment, such as criticism or withholding sex. Either you love me this way (which is right), or you don't love me at all (which is wrong). Controlling another person's acts of love by demanding love instead of desiring it is idolatry. A woman may hold onto this idol because she knows she is right, but in holding onto it, she becomes wrong.

Jolene, as many stated, "wore the pants in the family." She was extremely organized and worked hard for her family. She was intelligent, productive, and efficient. Kids arrived to sports on time or early, lunches were made, and the home was mostly clean. She was often disappointed and angry with her kids and husband when they failed to follow her instructions or meet her expectations. While the family appreciated her efforts, her relationships struggled as some members of the family did not feel they could meet her expectations. Jolene wanted her husband Cliff to love her by doing more around the house and spending time with her. When Cliff went golfing with his friends every Friday, she felt rejected and hurt because he chose to spend time apart from her. Jolene's relationship law was that Cliff had to be home when he was not working. If he broke her law, she criticized him for not loving her and withdrew her affection from him. While

Cliff agreed to skip one Friday per month to be with Jolene, he thought she was being selfish because he was home every day besides Friday. Jolene thought Cliff was being selfish for wanting to golf and not giving in to her desires.

Many Christians would understand this situation as his lack of understanding or follow through with her "love language." While it's true he can express love to her differently, he may lack an understanding of how to love her best. However, his commitment to stay home some Fridays is still a loving decision. The issue may occur when the black-and-white thinking wife learns her "love language" and demands he love her this way, and makes it worse when she sees this as "either he loves me by doing my love language, or he doesn't love me at all."

Let me suggest some questions for female black-and-white thinkers to ask themselves: What types of laws have you set in your heart for your home? For your children? If you're married, what if your husband showed his love for you in other ways? Do you dismiss his loving gestures as wrong or can you also accept his form of love as meaningful? What relationship laws have you set in your heart for your husband? How do you respond when you don't get what you want, or he does not obey your relational laws?

Men, Your Turn

The creation account in Genesis shows us that Adam desired companionship. God observed that it was not good that man was alone (Gen 2:18). Adam wanted to be *in* relationship even though man was not created for human relationship in the same way as a woman. Rather, Adam was created for work. God placed Adam in the garden of Eden to work it and care for it (Gen 2:5, 15).

Relationships, however, are an important and necessary means for both men and women to learn, grow, love, and become like Christ. Although women were created for relationship, they were created to be equal with man, and not for man to do as he wishes. If the black-and-white thinker believes that his spouse is created for him, to please him and make him happy, he is outside of God's plan for marriage. The same applies for wives as well. Such thinking is self-centered and not God-pleasing. Like women, male black-and-white thinkers also have "relationship laws." Their laws, however, are not about being loved but about being respected. When these desires become demands (from desiring respect to demanding it), the laws will become overbearing to spouses and may lead to emotional abuse. Scripture calls these laws idols of the heart. They become more important to receive than responding in ways that please God.

Sean was a foreman who worked outside on most days. He was admired by most employers and co-workers because he was a hard worker and he knew the business. If any of the workers became disrespectful, Sean would call them out. At home, Sean wasn't very different. When his wife said something he deemed disrespectful, he "corrected her" by raising his voice and telling her she was being disrespectful and expecting her to either apologize or be silent. If she argued with him, he spoke louder and called her names. He stated he wasn't going to put up with her disrespect, and either left the house or threatened to divorce her. Sean's relationship law was about being respected, and when this law was broken, his wife was punished. Sean saw himself as the victim of his wife's disrespect, but was unable to see that his wife was the victim of his unloving responses and verbal abuse.

Male black-and-white thinkers might ask themselves these questions: In what ways does your wife honor or serve you? Do you dismiss these ways as wrong? What relationship laws have you set in your heart? How do you respond when you don't get what you want?

The differences above are not meant to be comprehensive but provide a broad outline of areas where God has created men and women differently. For more on the male's desire for respect and a female's desire for love, read Ephesians 5. I also recommend the book, *Love and Respect* by Emerson Eggerichs. As with most books on relationships, there is a general caution we ought to keep in mind. Words can easily be twisted to meet our own wants, needs, or demands. Any person can understand that men generally want respect and women generally want love, however words can easily be twisted to say we need them and you need to give it to me. Such relationship books are resources for personal growth and change, not to control others or make them conform to your wants.

Relationship laws are essentially expectations and standards set for the other person. When unmet, they often result in criticisms, comments, or correction given to the other person. Additionally, relationship laws can also be idols in our hearts. When a simple desire for love or respect becomes a demand, then it becomes an idol. The focus on making the other person into your image of a perfect spouse created to make you happy or fulfilled is self-centered. However, our goal ought not to be about getting others to meet our standards, but for us to seek after Christ and be changed so that we become like Him—the full image of God.

There are similarities and differences between men and women black-and-white thinkers. Both live by standards and tend to create relational laws and activity laws for others. For men, the relational laws are about being respected, while women's laws tend to be about being loved. Both male and female black-and-white thinkers have activity laws where expectations are set for others regarding the quantity or quality of their performance. If these expectations remain unmet, both male and female black-and-white thinkers ought to be aware of their responses as God seeks to be glorified in all we do.

Reflection Questions:

1. What type of laws do you have in your life and relationships? Are they more relational laws or activity laws? How do you respond when such laws are broken?

2. What past struggles or traumas influence your laws for others? How have these past struggles or people from the past influenced such laws?

6

Practical Tips for Marriage

It is common for a black-and-white thinker to be married to a relational thinker. Such distinctions in marriage allow the strengths and weaknesses of each to complement one another, and at other times, cause division. Both come to the proverbial table with different values and perceptions, and both handle conflicts differently than the other. This chapter briefly addresses some of the common differences and how to address them.

Black-and-White Thinkers in Marriage

Those who are more rigid in their black-and-white thinking often struggle in relationships, while those who possess more relational traits do not struggle as much. More rigid black-and-white thinkers desire successful relationships but struggle due to their difficulty understanding and speaking relationally. In the mind of many black-and-white thinkers, a successful marriage is where both partners do what they're supposed to do, like a team. Many black-and-white thinkers, however, marry someone who has a different idea of what a successful marriage looks like. If you're a black-and-white thinker married to a relational thinker, here are a few tips to help you in your marriage:

Get Rid of Anger

Many black-and-white thinkers are most comfortable expressing anger, which is often a secondary emotion. Anger is what I consider a funnel emotion. That is, the emotions of hurt, fear, grief, sadness, etc., are often funneled into one emotion—anger. Anger is one of the greatest intimacy busters in relationships. When the expectations and standards we set for the other person are unmet, it often fuels anger. Harsh words, criticisms, complaints, and verbal and physical expressions of anger will harm a person so much emotionally that relationships often succumb to anger's oppression. If you want to improve your marriage, get rid of your unrighteous anger (Col 3:8 Eph 4:31–32). That requires dealing with heart demands, "needs," and underlying emotions. To get rid of the anger, explore and address the primary emotions under the anger. Challenge your underlying expectations and standards and learn how to receive and give grace. Grace is the unmerited favor we've received from God and ought to accept for ourselves and give to others. It is favoring and valuing the other person even though they did not meet a standard.

Jon was married to Susan for fifteen years. Since early in their marriage, he would become angry at Susan for many, many things. She did not speak to him respectfully. She was not grateful. She took another person's side and not his. She did not recognize his loving actions toward her. After years of feeling oppressed by his anger, Susan separated from Jon and refused to work on the relationship until he sought counseling for his anger. In counseling, Jon learned that his anger toward his wife stemmed from his desire to be accepted and loved by his father. He needed the approval of someone close to him, and when he did not get it from his wife, he became angry and punished her with his words. Upon this realization, Jon humbled himself and forgave his father for his high standards, turned to God for his sense of value and personal worth, and repented to his wife. Humbling himself and acknowledging his deepest heart needs and meeting them through Christ were the first steps Jon took to get rid of his anger. Anger cannot be removed by simply changing behaviors, but through the Holy Spirit changing the heart.

Intimacy Over Actions

Emotions and feelings are abstract and therefore difficult for many black-and-white thinkers to grasp. Yet it is necessary to acknowledge and even feel emotions. Two steps will help you grow in your intimacy with your spouse. The first is to understand your spouse's feelings and thoughts, and the second is the ability to express yours.

One of my favorite lines in the Prayer of St. Francis is "Not to be understood, but to understand. Not to be loved but to love." St.

Francis prayed that his focus would not be on himself, but instead on the other person. The goal of intimacy is to understand and value another's thoughts, feelings, and desires above our own.

Proverbs 20:5 states that "The purposes of a person's heart are deep waters, but one who has insight [understanding] draws them out." If we are to understand what is in the hearts of others, we need to pay close attention, not assume motives, and then go deeper.

Keep these four levels of communication in mind: Cliché, Facts, Thoughts, and Feelings. The deeper you go in communication, the deeper the intimacy within the relationship. Why? Because the thoughts, desires, and feelings are the heart of a person. A heart's desires and motives are central to our relationship with Him and others. The heart is where many people feel connected to others, and where God connects with us. God desires our whole hearts be fully committed to Him as evidenced by our thoughts and actions (Mt 22:37). We become more intimate with God when we spend time seeking His perspectives, wants, and desires with all our hearts (Mt 6:33). This demonstrates our love for Him by paying attention and declaring His wants are important to us. Intimacy with your spouse is not much different. The deeper we go in understanding our spouse's thoughts, desires, and feelings, the deeper and greater our intimacy will be with them. Consider the following illustration:

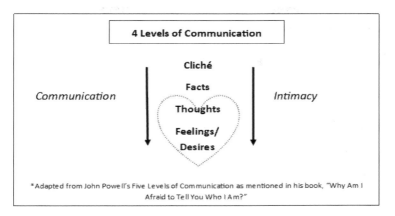

4 Levels of Communication

Communication

Intimacy

Cliché

Facts

Thoughts

Feelings/
Desires

*Adapted from John Powell's Five Levels of Communication as mentioned in his book, "Why Am I Afraid to Tell You Who I Am?"

The more you focus on knowing the thoughts, desires, and feelings of your spouse, and the more you accept them and value them, the more connected your spouse will feel.

Many black-and-white thinkers struggle to go deeper than facts, much to the disappointment of their spouse. Disagreements occur because the other person's facts are wrong, and the conversation becomes about what facts are correct and which are not. At times, the facts lead to a tangent about what the person could do, when they would prefer to simply be listened to and valued. When conversations are about facts and fixes, thoughts and feelings may never be approached. The heart is never touched which can be frustrating for the spouse. If thoughts or feelings are expressed, they may be dismissed because the black-and-white thinker believes they are either unimportant or inaccurate because the facts are not accurate. While it is true that facts can change our perspectives and feelings about a situation, addressing facts or fixes prematurely will often end in disappointment and conflict.

The relational thinker will feel that their heart was not heard, and the black-and-white thinker will feel like their advice is not being heard. When this occurs, both communication and intimacy remain shallow.

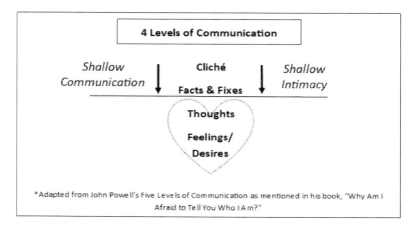

*Adapted from John Powell's Five Levels of Communication as mentioned in his book, "Why Am I Afraid to Tell You Who I Am?"

I am reminded of the online video about the woman with a nail in her head. She desperately wants her husband to know how she feels about this pain while he just wants to fix her problem by telling her she needs to remove the nail. After some minor arguing, he relents and listens to her feelings. She feels valued by him because he listened without fixing her, but she still had the nail in her head. While this is an exaggerated and humorous example, it doesn't fall far from the goal of listening to the heart.

To grow in intimacy, it is important to prioritize the thoughts and feelings of the other person over the importance of the facts. Facts ought not to be ignored but seen as secondary in importance to thoughts and feelings. The most challenging part in understanding another's feeling is to understand the impact of one's sins upon the other. At times, we may hurt others deeply, causing deeper pain and fear, but we fail to realize the impact of our sins. Taking time to do listen and reflect on the impact of your own sins upon another can lead to healing in relationships, especially when genuine repentance follows. When another's thoughts and feelings are valued and understood, you are entering the deep waters of emotional intimacy.

Closeness with your spouse is more likely to occur when you choose to believe the motives of your spouse rather than ascribing motives. When we say things such as, "you did this because ..." or "you're just feeling sorry for yourself," or "you are just being selfish," we are ascribing motives. We assume we know their hearts, but in reality, we are being prideful and arrogant. We believe we understand their hearts and whatever they say is not true. Some may even accuse the spouse of lying. Intimacy improves when we are humble in our interpretation and refuse to believe ourselves over our spouses.

Growing in intimacy must first start with understanding and valuing your spouse's thoughts, feelings, and desires, then—and only then—is it important to express your own. Expressing your own emotions without listening or valuing your spouse's emotions first shows them your emotions are the only ones that matter. Theirs do not.

41

Chances are your spouse wants to connect with you. However, their connection to you will not be the same way you desire to connect. Your spouse will likely need to feel connected to you at the heart level. When you value and understand their perspective and hurts without passing judgment, the connection between you will likely grow. Relational spouses desire couple intimacy (into-me-see) over couple efficiency (working well together). If you want a better marriage with a relational spouse, you'll also need to understand yourself better so that you can share your own heart. Of course, accomplishing this requires emotional vulnerability—a very attractive quality to a relational spouse when expressed honestly and humbly.

After his humility and repentance, Jon learned how to connect better with his wife's heart. Instead of interrupting his wife, he listened to her patiently. In the past, Jon would correct her facts and argue with her points. Now Jon learned to listen for her emotions, fears, and desires. Jon did not offer advice, but sought to understand better without making judgments and ask her what he could do for her. Jon was beginning to learn how to connect with his wife in a way she needed.

Shift Tactics: Be Vulnerable

Since the operating system of the black-and-white thinker is all or nothing, right or wrong, and either-or, black-and-white thinkers ought to acknowledge that their thinking does not work well for the intimacy their spouse desires. They will often show their love for their spouses by doing things around the house—chores or other projects to make their spouse happy. Even though these things may be appreciated, they often miss the mark of reaching the heart. Additionally, black-and-white thinkers will often complain or criticize the relational person for being difficult to please. They may think, "If my spouse is annoyed, they're annoyed at me because they think I did something wrong. I try to do what she wants, but she is still annoyed. I can't do anything right in her eyes."

If this is the case, you may express your love in actions, but the intimacy your relational spouse desires won't be achieved through acts of service or sex. Intimacy requires a heart connection. A heart connection is made when you are vulnerable. Think about your fears, sorrows, and desires. Then share them. Before you share, however, seek to know and understand your spouse's fears, sorrows, and desires to the best of your ability. If you have hurt your spouse deeply, you may need to focus on understanding and valuing your spouse's hurts and hearts for a long period of time before they are ready to listen to yours. Acknowledge them and value them by allowing them to influence your actions. If the black-and-white thinker recognizes the need for this shift in approach and understands that their acts of service are ineffective for intimacy, they've taken a step toward a better relationship with their spouse. Don't stop those acts of service! They, too, are a good way to show your love. But they don't qualify for intimacy.

Seek Wisdom Above All Else

Black-and-white thinkers often think moralistically, meaning they see things as right and wrong or good and bad. They generally interpret actions, words, and situations as right or wrong. I challenge black-and-white thinkers to confront their own thinking. Instead of declaring actions and words as right or wrong, or good or bad, try shifting the question from, "Is it right or wrong?" to "Is it wise?" I remember hearing a sermon once where the pastor challenged the congregation to ask themselves, "What would a wise person do or say? How would a wise person respond?" Then do it. Ultimately, this is another way of asking the cliché question, "What would Jesus do?" as Jesus is the wisdom of God (1 Cor 1:24). When Jesus encountered the adulterous woman in John 8, He took time to ponder before replying. Then, without condemning the woman, Jesus responded mercifully to her while acknowledging right and wrong at the same time. Additionally, he communicated to everyone ready to judge that they have their own sins to worry about. Those surrounding the adulterous woman were so busy being right according to the law, they missed the obvious truth that they have not always been right either. True wisdom is not simply declaring right or wrong, but considering the relational qualities of mercy and grace for others as well.

Becoming Like Jesus

For the black-and-white thinker, the importance of meeting standards or expectations is paramount. But lacking the relational components, such as grace, mercy, compassion, kindness, and empathy, relationships will suffer. Jesus, who met every standard by God perfectly, yet full of grace, did not come to "abolish the law" but fulfilled it. He fulfilled the law by being perfectly obedient to it, yet he also fully loved and valued people for who they are, not for what they've done. He even did so on the road to the cross. Consider these facts about Jesus and the cross:

1. Although Jesus was always right, he was willing to go to the cross and be treated as though he were wrong because He loved people. His goal was not to be right or make sure others believed he was right. Instead, he simply spoke truth and loved people where they were.

2. Jesus was willing to be treated unfairly. His deeds deserved honor, not crucifixion. He was willing to do this to pay the penalty of our sins. He took what we deserved upon himself.

3. Jesus treated others unfairly. He treated his oppressors unfairly by asking the Father to forgive them, not smite them. Why? Because he loved even his oppressors and us!

45

In the Gospels, Jesus is not only the model for black-and-white thinkers, but he is the Savior of black-and-white thinkers and relational thinkers alike. God desires to conform us to the likeness of Christ (Rom 8:29). This ought to also be our goal as black-and-white thinkers. To become like Christ, we must confess our sinfulness, recognize our need for Christ, humble ourselves, and cooperate with the Holy Spirit to grow in the grace and knowledge of our Lord and Savior, Jesus Christ (2 Pet 3:18). Cultivating successful relationships requires us to become more like Jesus, to love like Jesus, and value others like Jesus. As we do so, our marriages change.

Many people try hard to make their marriages work, but in trying harder, they often repeat the same patterns. Not all marriages will change if we simply try harder, but many do change when we try *differently*. If you are a black-and-white thinker, consider getting rid of your anger, seeking heart connection (intimacy) over actions, being humble and vulnerable, and cooperating with the Holy Spirit to gain the relational qualities of Jesus. If you work at these things, your marriage is bound to improve.

Married to a Black-and-White Thinker

Marriage is both a beautiful picture of the greater union between Christ and the Church, and a complicated mess because of our sinful nature, intrinsic differences, and cultural influences.

46

Most people would agree we choose partners who are different than us. They possess traits we don't. They may complement our weaknesses or strengths, and we complement theirs. The thinking that once endeared a relational person to the black-and-white thinker—their concrete, clear thinking, straight talk, confidence—soon is seen as a frustrating weakness. The relational thinker may have been looking for a close relationship, only to find that this is a struggle. The more black-and-white thinking a spouse possesses, the more difficult the struggle for a deeper relationship becomes.

With these things in mind, here are some things to keep in mind if you're married to a black-and-white thinker.

Taking Offense

"No offense, but you're ugly." This is one of the little games we'd play with my peers when I was in third grade. We'd start of by saying, "no offense" followed by something offensive. Taking offense at other's words and actions often leads to hurt, resentment, and often some form of revenge. Holding onto offense is so destructive in our walk with God and others, pastor and author Paul Bevere calls it "the bait of Satan." In fact, he wrote a book using this very phrase. If we take offense to another's words and actions, Satan has his foothold in us, and sin will certainly follow.

As previously discussed, black-and-white thinkers are standard-makers. They often hold people to certain standards in their minds which eventually comes out of their mouths. Comments and criticisms are made about a person who fails to achieve a standard or meet an expectation. This is common in close relationships and it often is the reason why people become offended.

Offense is often taken when someone says something insensitive or acts in selfish or uncaring ways. Criticisms in private or in public can cause feelings to be hurt and trust to be broken. When it is done by someone you love, the hurt is deeper still. Left unaddressed, such hurts will continue if you remain silent or if your spouse does not hear your heart.

Addressing and responding to such hurts in respectful or loving ways will be important so the offense is not held in the heart. At times, you may need to be respectful, yet firm in sharing how you've been offended. If you believe you are being dismissed, you may need to share this and ask them if their intent was to hurt you. If not, share how it hurt you and ask them to commit to refrain from such words or acts in the future.

At times, offense is taken because we have misinterpreted the words of another as well. I remember a time attending a church event at a congregant's house when all I wanted to do was sit with friends. My wife approached me in front of my friends and asked me if I was having a good time, because she was watching the kids. I immediately became offended and began to defend myself because what I heard her say was that I was being selfish and was being a bad father. Therefore, I decided I would not speak to her the rest of the night to punish her for her disrespect. Then the Lord convicted me, "You're a counselor. What would you tell a client in this situation?" Well, I would tell a client to approach your wife and ask her the reasons behind the statement. So, I listened to this voice and asked my wife what she meant. She just wanted to let me know she was watching the kids so I could have a good time with my friends. I took offense because I interpreted her words incorrectly. If you find yourself taking offense, you may need to clarify your spouse's intent behind their words and actions.

At times, black-and-white thinkers are stating facts that are not intended as criticisms, nor are their words meant to be taken as criticisms. Now, certain facts certainly don't need to be stated, especially facts that are less endearing to a person. Stating such facts are often unnecessary and will hurt a more sensitive person. Yet we are responsible for how we interpret the words and can choose to be offended, or choose not to be offended. Yes, it's a choice!

If you were to take an inventory of the heart, would you find offense in it? If so, I strongly urge you to take some time with the Lord, seek His forgiveness for holding onto it, and seek his strength, wisdom, and discernment on responding to careless and offensive statements.

Expectations

If you're more relational, it's important to know that black-and-white thinkers are not like you, nor should they be expected to be. They will process things differently, and they may struggle with loving you, but not because of you. The more black-and-white their thinking is, the more they will struggle with the nuances of relational dynamics or the emotions of those closest to them. If they seek to do better in relationships, it may be helpful to understand relationship rules such as, if someone is doing A, you do B in response. However, this ability does not come naturally to them. Unfortunately, the black-and-white thinker may find it difficult to understand the emotional impact of their actions upon their spouse or children. This is especially true for those who are ruled by pride. Those who humble themselves can learn what to do if communication breaks down and work to improve relationships.

Love

Love can be both feelings-driven and fact-based. Relational thinkers often show their love for their spouse based on emotions and feelings. While there will be loving actions based on duty or responsibilities, many times the emotions inside drive love itself. Love may flow from the emotions of gratitude, joy, being in love, or similar emotions, or simply because they feel like it. For relational thinkers, emotions are often a springboard for love.

Many black-and-white thinkers lean toward expressing love in more tangible ways with less emotional heart connection. For many black-and-white thinkers, love is fact-based. Their demonstrations of love may be more like acts of service, such as taking care of your car, doing projects around the house, or making you dinner. The spontaneous feelings of love may not drive their loving actions, but outward behaviors often demonstrate their love and commitment.

Black-and-white thinking Christians show their love for God in the same way. Loving God flows out of obedience—driven by their sense of what is right and good. I believe God accepts this as their acts of love. If your spouse loves you because it is good, right, and it pleases you, then you can learn to accept it as expressed. This can be difficult for many spouses because there is a strong desire to connect emotionally with a spouse. It is a struggle to accept the depth of intimacy that is longed for may not occur, or at least, not to the level that is desired.

Keep in mind that your spouse may not speak your "love language" or be emotionally vulnerable with you or emotionally available to you. Such "failures" do not mean they don't love you. They may express their love through doing things for you, as opposed to identifying with your emotions and connecting with you at the heart level as you desire. You may need to draw nearer to God and find other people of the same sex to connect with emotionally, or you may find couples counseling helpful to connect at the heart level.

Sharon was a personal friend of mine before cancer quickened her journey home to heaven. Her husband, a black-and-white thinker, was a good man, but struggled relationally to connect with her. While her heart longed for that connection with him, she learned what it meant to have Jesus as her husband. The intimacy with Jesus that grew during this time filled her with a joy she never knew. She shared with me a time when she was on her porch praying intimately to God when a bird landed on her arm. She instantly knew that was the Lord letting her know he was there with her. Then the bird pooped on her arm. She laughed and stated, "That was the Lord letting me know he has a sense of humor."

Draw nearer to God if you don't presently connect with your spouse emotionally. Let Him fill you with His love as a daughter or son in whom He finds joy and favor. It is His love that gives you value and worth, not your spouse's, parents' or child's love, but His alone.

Conflict

Conflict often occurs when two people disagree about what is right or wrong. But when there is conflict between a relational thinker and a black-and-white thinker, each views the situation from a different perspective. "Right" for a relational person means being considerate of the feelings and emotions of the person and making the relationship a priority. In the black-and-white thinker's mind, "right" may be what matches their standard or expectation. If you break the rule or don't meet their expectation, punishment must be enforced. In both situations, whatever is right may be defined by personal desires that have turned into demands. A relational thinker may argue, "You need to give the kids a break from doing their chores! You're a tyrant!" A black-and-white thinker may argue, "You can't let the kids off the hook from doing what they should be doing. They need to be responsible, and you're too soft!" While teaching responsibility is important, showing grace and mercy to your children is also important if you wish to have a relationship that is not built solely on works. At times it will be better to consider the relationship rather than be right. At other times we will need to be in the right and not be concerned with others' feelings. Working together to discern what to do and when is of utmost importance as too much of either side will cause damage to the relationship and the outcome.

Warnings

When pride and self-centeredness reign in a black-and-white thinker's life (see Chap. 7), the marriage cannot be healthy. Genuine reconciliation becomes nearly impossible. "I'm not perfect" is not an acknowledgment of wrong. When a person makes this excuse, they are not admitting fault, reconciling, or loving sincerely. Mutuality is nonexistent. When the focus of the black-and-white thinker is on self and not on what is good for others, they may try to control others with their anger. They do what they think is best and try to get others to do the same, often using the Scriptures to manipulate the spouse. These is narcissistic behaviors and ruins relationships. A narcissistic marriage is emotionally destructive. In such cases, it is wise to seek help from a Christian counselor. Two wise counselors who address emotionally destructive relationships are Leslie Vernick (www.leslievernick.com) and Chris Moles (www.chrismoles.org). They each do a fantastic job speaking into emotionally destructive marriages and providing biblical counsel to those involved in such relationships.

One of the greatest struggles for a person married to a black-and-white thinker who is abusive is to make a stand for their spouse and against their sin. Many relational thinkers can be people pleasers who are afraid of conflict. Some enable their spouses to continue to sin by not addressing the sin. Making a stand for your spouse means to speak against the sin and may involve consequences for actions. You act on their behalf by letting them know that it is not alright to sin against you, because they are sinning against God, too. It is beyond the scope of this book to dig deeper into abuse in marriage. I would recommend exploring the websites listed in the previous paragraph for wisdom in addressing abuse further.

Hope

Many relational thinkers are married to black-and-white thinkers. However, when partners recognize the differences and strengths in the other, they can humbly get through them together. Even if one is not willing to work, help is not too far away. Change is possible if someone *wants* to change. For some in abusive situations, a relationship crisis, such as a separation or threat of separation may be necessary. Rock bottom can be a good foundation to build on! For others, it may be as simple as a sit-down conversation stating that you are upset with the status quo and asking for things to change. For those who are not in crisis, making minor changes in your expectations and educating yourself about the differences may begin the change process. You may need to accept and appreciate that God has given you a black-and-white thinking spouse to help you become more like Him.

As a relational thinker married to a black-and-white thinker, I am amazed at how perfect we are for one another. My wife is organized, a researcher and planner, hard worker, and efficient. In fact, she is so efficient, she completed our desire to have two kids with one pregnancy (Yes, we have twins!). Now that's efficient! I complement my wife by being more laid back, enjoying and encouraging relationships, and being the comic relief in order to keep things light. While we butt heads occasionally, we recognize these times reflect our strengths and weaknesses simultaneously. She sees my laid back as being lazy (and I can be lazy!). I see her always being busy as working too hard (and sometimes it is!). When we come together, search our hearts and try to understand what occurred, we understand where our differences came into play. She's not wrong or bad. She's just different. I'm not necessarily wrong either. I'm just different than her. And sometimes we're both wrong because sin is present. What strengths attracted us to each other are also the weaknesses that may cause conflicts. Even so, God can use these strengths and weaknesses to help conform us to the likeness of Christ. Individually, we only do so much. But together, we are an effective ministry team.

Remember, even though God is relational, God also sees things in black-and-white. While we are all created in His image, reflecting different aspects of Him is a good thing. Working together to reflect Him as one is also good—challenging—but good. I hope this will help you understand your spouse better and challenge you to accept certain aspects of his or her interpretive lens as a strength and not as weakness or incompetence. Additionally, I hope this information will challenge you to work on your own heart and develop a greater intimacy with your spouse.

Reflection Questions:

1. Are you a black-and-white thinker married to a relational thinker? Are you beginning to understand how you are different? Will you challenge yourself to listen to your spouse's heart and thoughts without trying to fix or correct? Will you offer praise and reduce or eliminate criticism? Will you work to become more vulnerable?

2. Are you a relational thinker married to a black-and-white thinker? Do you get offended by their words or actions? How will you keep from holding on to an offense? Will you recognize their love shown to you as love and accept it as such? Will you work together with your spouse, recognizing that the black-and-white thinking reflects God (albeit tainted by sin?) Will you gently confront sin and speak up for the person, but against sin?

7

When Pride Reigns

Let's be honest. We're all prideful. I'm not talking about taking-pride-in-our-work kind of pride. No, I'm talking about the self-centered, self-aggrandizing, self-focused, all-about-me kind of pride. The kind of self-centeredness that all of us have inside, thanks to the sinful nature we have inherited from Adam and Eve.

Our pride and self-centeredness manifest themselves in different ways. At times they occur in subtle ways that nobody notices, such as in our unspoken thoughts. At other times they can be disguised in our kindness to others, while we act covertly for our own benefit. Still, at other times, our self-centered pride is evident in our speech and actions.

While pride is present in everyone, we all seem to have one or two areas where it shows up more frequently. In their book, *Relationships: A Mess Worth Making*, authors Paul Tripp and Tim Lane describe six areas of pride in our lives. They include:

- self-centeredness—seeking attention and approval
- self-rule—seeking to be right or to be in control
- self-sufficiency—seeking independence

- self-satisfaction—seeking pleasure
- self-righteousness—seeking to be right in the eyes of others; and
- self-taught—seeking to give an opinion.[2]

The first time I read this list I knew that I possessed all six areas of pride in my life, with some areas are greater than others. Sadly, it's not very different now. There's a good chance that you may be like me. Pride follows us wherever we go and rears its ugly head when we least expect it.

As previously mentioned, black-and-white thinkers simplify their judgments into whatever is good or bad, and right or wrong. When pride is present, *admitting* wrong is often tantamount to *being* wrong or bad. And if you *can't* be wrong, then you must be right, and others are wrong. To admit to being wrong may be a significant blow to the black-and-white thinker's esteem, which may be fragile. When pride governs the black-and-white thinker, self-righteousness and self-rule are often the two most difficult heart struggles on the list. The need to be right and appear right to others lends itself to making justifications, excuses, and blame. Doing so convinces black-and-white thinkers and others they are in the right and others are in the wrong. We all do this, relational thinkers and black-and-white thinkers alike. However, when pride reigns in the black-and-white thinker's heart, the justifications, blaming, and excuses are regular occurrences. Additionally, if

, considered *good* and being *wrong* is considered *bad*,

ndency to look at oneself as better and others as worse

nemonstrated in bragging, insults, and criticisms.

,. 've noted that black-and-white thinkers are likened to the Pharisees in Scripture who obey the law. That is, anyone who falls short of their standard deserves punishment. The Pharisees started with God's law and then added over 600 written laws plus additional oral laws so they would not violate the original law. When black-and-white thinkers make their own laws or standards in their homes and expect others to follow them, they can become controlling through criticism and conflicts. They may look down on others who don't measure up. Controlling comments and behaviors like anger or rage occur in emotionally or physically abusive relationships.

Of course, it is important to note that abusive relationships are more likely to occur when pride dominates in black-and-white thinkers, not simply if pride is present. Pride is evidence of our fallen humanity. When pride holds sway in our lives, we are completely absorbed in ourselves, and we are moving toward what psychologists call narcissism. To keep pride from governing our hearts, we must recognize that we are sinful and that it is quite normal to be wrong. That doesn't mean that we are to pursue wrongdoing, of course, but to expect it as fallen human beings. Our wrongness, per se, does not impact our value or worth as humans, but it does help us recognize our need for Christ and his great love for us, which is not based on our wrongdoing. This is the path to humility. As we recognize our sinfulness and seek Christ, He begins to change us inwardly so that pride does not rule in our hearts.

Karl could not see or understand that he emotionally abused his wife, but instead saw himself as the victim of a bad marriage. He found fault in his wife's cooking, body, lovemaking, and the way she raised the kids. He often brought these things up to her to try to help her become a better mother and spouse. He even turned to portions of Scripture, he reasoned, to teach and admonish his wife so she would be obedient to God. He referenced 1 Corinthians 7:4-5 so she would not give in to selfishness by denying him her body when he desired sex. He quoted a portion of Ephesians 5:22 to get her to submit to his will because that is what God wants. When she didn't listen, he became angry and called her a bad Christian amidst a tirade of other names. He even threatened to divorce her, hoping she would change. Eventually, Karl's wife shut down and left him when another man showed interest in her.

What Karl didn't realize was that he was trying to create his wife into the image of what a perfect wife should be in his mind, and he did not accept or love her for who she was. He manipulated the Word of God to get what he wanted and refused to consider the meanings behind such passages or pay attention to what he ought to do. Karl was a king in his own kingdom and saw his wife as his servant who existed for him. He saw her as someone who existed to make his life happy and successful, but he could not see that his role, according to Scripture, was to serve his wife.

One illustration I have found helpful in counseling is using the coined diagnosis called "King Syndrome." King Syndrome is simply the belief that I am king or queen in my life. My way is best. I am right. I want what I want when I want it. My goals, my wants, my opinions, my dreams, my needs and my happiness are more important than anyone else's, and they ought to be most important to others as well. Some people would call this acting like a baby. The Scriptures call this our sinful nature. For illustration purposes, I am calling this King (or Queen) Syndrome.

As kings or queens, we live in our castles (homes), own our chariots (automobiles), and are surrounded by servants (family) and peasants (co-workers, people in the community) who exist to make our lives better—to meet our desires for a successful life.

What is a successful life? Perhaps it is having something you wish you had as a child, such as better finances, a marriage that doesn't end in divorce, or to be treated better than your father treated your mother, or mother treated your father. Perhaps it is something different altogether. If another's actions do not measure up to such standards or get in the way of the successful life, they often receive the wrath of the king so they will "get in line" with the wants of the king.

Is your desire for fully obedient children (servants), yet they don't listen to you the first time? Yell at them and punish them so they fear you. They deserve your wrath. Is your spouse (servant) not doing what you think they should? Criticize them or call them names so they will fear you and will do what you want next time. Caught behind a slow driver (peasant)? Honk your horn and yell at them. Give them what they deserve! The wrath of the king falls only on deserving people. After all, it is their actions that caused the wrath, right?

Wrong. Scripture always point to the heart. Not other's hearts, but our own hearts (Lk 6:45). Others do not make us respond in certain ways, but we respond to their actions based on what is in our hearts, whether good or evil. When we see ourselves as kings or queens in our own kingdoms and others as servants or peasants, we may eventually lose our relationships through pain and conflict. Many people struggle to recognize this, but instead believe others are wrong, and everything will be better when they do what we think they should do. This rarely, if ever, happens. In fact, it often creates more distance.

Have you ever told yourself, "I can't believe I did that" or "I can't believe I didn't see this earlier"? Well, why not? Do we think we are so righteous we are not capable of doing wrong or so knowledgeable we shouldn't miss anything? Often times, we can't see such things because pride blinds us to truth. Its presence is the reason we don't see what we're doing is wrong. It is the reason we turn a blind eye to our own sins, but recognize sin's presence in other's lives. It is the reason we can't believe we did something wrong or didn't see things earlier. Pride is the greatest enemy of relationships with God and others. If our relationships are going to be successful, our pride and selfishness need to be confronted.

Change is not about changing behaviors; it is about changing kingdoms. We need to remove the imaginary crowns from our heads and place the real crown on the head of Christ through repentance. When Christ is king, we become his servants. This is the mindset and heart posture that is necessary for followers of Christ.

The Lord's Prayer (Matt 6:9–13) is all about changing kingdoms. It is a recognition that He is God, that we are in His kingdom, and we are dependent on Him. Read this prayer carefully a few times:

Our father in heaven, hallowed be your name, your kingdom come, your will be done on earth as it is in heaven. Give us today our daily bread; and forgive us our debts as we also have forgiven our debtors. And lead us not into temptation, but deliver us from the evil one.

Now read it again. The Lord's Prayer is a prayer of humility from a servant and child of the Father and King. As servants in His kingdom, our hearts are for His kingdom on earth. Our mouths express words of encouragement and love reflecting His kingdom.

Our hands are used for His kingdom purposes. Our minds are focused on His kingdom concerns. People no longer exist to be our servants, but we exist to become their servants because we serve God by loving others as ourselves (Lk 10:27).

Pride is present in all of us, but when we allow pride to reign in our hearts, our love for self grows while love for God and others diminishes. We cannot simply become humble, but we can humble ourselves through repentance and kingdom change. Let Christ be king and let us be his servants. It is the only way.

If this is something you struggle with, get down in a humble posture before God and confess this to Him. Ask God to change this heart of stone into a heart of flesh (Ez 36:26). Ask Him to give you the heart of a servant and the mindset to see others in your life as people who don't exist for you, but who exist for you to love and serve.

Consider these wise thoughts by Nancy Leigh DeMoss between proud and broken people:

Proud people focus on the failures of others.
Broken people are overwhelmed with a sense of their own spiritual need.

Proud people have a critical, fault-finding spirit; they look at everyone else's faults with a microscope but their own with a telescope.
Broken people are compassionate; they can forgive much because they know how much they have been forgiven.

Proud people are self-righteous; they look down on others.
Broken people esteem all others better than themselves.

65

Proud people have an independent, self-sufficient spirit.
Broken people have a dependent spirit; they recognize their need for others.

Proud people have to prove that they are right.
Broken people are willing to yield the right to be right.

Proud people are self-protective of their time, their rights, and their reputation.
Broken people are self-denying.

Proud people desire to be served.
Broken people are motivated to serve others.

Proud people desire self-advancement.
Broken people desire to promote others.

Proud people have a drive to be recognized and appreciated.
Broken people have a sense of their own unworthiness; they are thrilled that God would use them at all.

Proud people feel confident in how much they know.
Broken people are humbled by how very much they have to learn.

Proud people keep others at arms' length.
Broken people are willing to risk getting close to others and to take risks of loving intimately.

Proud people are quick to blame others.
Broken people accept personal responsibility and can see where they are wrong in a situation.

Proud people are unapproachable or defensive when criticized.
Broken people receive criticism with a humble, open spirit.

Proud people are concerned with being respectable, with what others think; they work to protect their own image and

reputation.
Broken people are concerned with being real; what matters to them is not what others think but what God knows; they are willing to die to their own reputation.

Proud people find it difficult to share their spiritual need with others.
Broken people are willing to be open and transparent with others as God directs.

Proud people want to be sure that no one finds out when they have sinned; their instinct is to cover up.
Broken people, once broken, don't care who knows or who finds out; they are willing to be exposed because they have nothing to lose.

Proud people have a hard time saying, "I was wrong; will you please forgive me?"
Broken people are quick to admit failure and to seek forgiveness when necessary.

Proud people tend to deal in generalities when confessing sin.
Broken people are able to acknowledge specifics when confessing their sin.

Proud people are concerned about the consequences of their sin.
Broken people are grieved over the cause, the root of their sin.

Proud people are remorseful over their sin, sorry that they got found out or caught.
Broken people are truly, genuinely repentant over their sin, evidenced in the fact that they forsake that sin.

Proud people wait for the other to come and ask forgiveness when there is a misunderstanding or conflict in a relationship.
Broken people take the initiative to be reconciled when there is misunderstanding or conflict in relationships; they race to

the cross; they see if they can get there first, no matter how wrong the other may have been.

Proud people compare themselves with others and feel worthy of honor.
Broken people compare themselves to the holiness of God and feel a desperate need for His mercy.

Proud people are blind to their true heart condition.
Broken people walk in the light.

Proud people don't think they have anything to repent of.
Broken people realize they have need of a continual heart attitude of repentance.[3]

After reading this list, how would you rate yourself? Do you find yourself having more in common with a proud person or a broken person? Solomon warns us in Proverbs 16:18 that "Pride comes before destruction; a haughty spirit before a fall." Pride is our enemy. Do all that is necessary to eradicate it from your life through confession and dependence on Him.

God opposes the proud, but gives grace to the humble.
—James 4:6, Prov 29:23

Reflection Questions:

1. How is King or Queen Syndrome most reflected in your life? What happens when your servants or peasants don't meet your expectations? What does the king or queen's wrath look like?

2. Look at the proud/brokenness list again by Nancy Leigh DeMoss. What three areas would you like to work on first? Pray for brokenness.

3. Ask God to change your heart from a heart of stone to a heart of flesh. Ask Him to help you see people the way He sees people, to love people the way He loves them.

8

Insecurity and Worth

We've likely all faced insecurity at one time or another. It doesn't matter who you are, how you were raised, your personality, ethnicity, or sex. Self-doubt, lacking confidence in who you are, and uncertainty of personal value and worth often echo in the back of our minds. Whether we've faced insecurity from time to time or as an everyday battle, insecurity will influence our reactions and relationships.

Where does our sense of security and worth come from? We first look to our parents for security. From birth to childhood we look to our parents for all of our basic needs: food, clothing, shelter, and yes, worth. Later we derive our value from peers and perhaps our performance. If our peers like and accept us, or our performance in academics, sports, or the arts garner us recognition and praise, we feel good about ourselves and believe we have value. While we can generally function well when our sense of security is found in only one or two of these areas, if our security in all three areas is lacking, our worth and value are compromised. We may even grow older continuing to seek worth and approval by continuing to perform well and please parents, peers, or even our spouses, but eventually, performance and people pleasing backfire in relationships. Our worth, however, is not found in the opinions of parents or peers, nor is it found in our performance – but it is found in God's opinion of you, and Christ's performance for you on the cross. Battling insecurity begins with recognizing God's truth. He loves you so much, He sent His one and only Son to die for you (Jn 3:16).

For insecure black-and-white thinkers, all-or-nothing thinking plays a significant role in interpreting both conversation and events. Insecure individuals have a difficult time distinguishing between behaviors and personhood. If you do something bad, this means you are a bad person. And if you are bad, then your sense of worth decreases. (We'll discuss negative self-worth and its role in depression in a later chapter.)

An insecure person generally takes things personally or get offended easily. They may take instruction or direction as criticism. When another person says the black-and-white thinker didn't do something well, they interpret it as meaning they did horrible. If someone tells the black-and-white thinker they did a good job, the black-and-white thinker may interpret the word 'good' as either 'great' or 'terrible.' It may be seen as terrible because they didn't use the word 'great' – like getting a B on a test. It typically goes to either extreme. There is no middle ground for many black-and-white thinkers.

Responsibility and Protection

For some black-and-white thinkers, accepting responsibility for wrong actions admits fault. Admitting fault or guilt would mean they are bad, horrible, no good and worthless—a reflection on their personhood. It means they are entirely to blame for the issue. To protect themselves, some use blame-shifting, justifying ("I yelled because you disrespected me!"), and may even attack others to keep their fragile personhood intact. For example, if you try to tell a black-and-white thinker that they did something wrong in a conflict, it is quite possible that they will think you are blaming them for the entire conflict and may demand that you take some responsibility, too. Why? Because they are either all to blame or not at all to blame. If they are all to blame, they are all bad or wrong. There may not be any middle ground. To take responsibility or admit guilt or wrongdoing only for their part, which may be only a portion of the conflict, may be difficult for them to grasp. So, either they may become significantly more depressed or more verbally aggressive. Such behavior does not occur in all black-and-white thinkers, only in those who struggle with insecurity.

Sean came to counseling struggling with depression. After some discussion and exploration into his relationships, he stated his wife Ginny has never admitted to being wrong. He often feels responsible for the problems in the marriage because she blames him. When he speaks to her about her actions that hurt him, she twists things around so that it seems he is to blame and needs to change. Sean leaves these conversations thinking he is either a bad person or he is going crazy. When Ginny agreed to come to counseling, we learned she grew up in a broken home where her father left before Ginny was born. Ginny was raised by a strong mom who was resentful of Ginny and her dad who left, so she was hard on her. Ginny learned not to take any garbage from any man, but to be independent. Ginny, however, deeply longed for love and acceptance. She could not accept blame because she blamed herself for her father's leaving, and any blame she felt took her back to the rejection by her parents. Ginny was insecure, but on the surface she presented as a very independent and secure woman.

Self-protection and preservation are the key tasks of an insecure black-and-white thinker. Often, feelings of hurt, rejection, grief, and abandonment are too difficult to bear. Because black-and-white thinkers are more concrete, and feelings are abstract, working through such intangible feelings seems like an impossible task. Additionally, since such negative feelings are both difficult and painful, their black-and-white thinking may escalate to simplify life and nullify their feelings. It's almost as if the protection mantra is this, "If the feelings aren't acknowledged or felt, they are not there. They don't exist." Life is simpler without emotions. Painful feelings are minimized, and concrete words and actions become more of a focus.

Healing often begins when the negative emotions of hurt, rejection, and abandonment are acknowledged and worked through rather than ignored. Such efforts are more effective after the individual first recognizes that their emotional security—their identity, self-worth, and value—rests in God's love and Christ's actions on the cross and not on what others have said or done, or in their performance. It's best to work through such emotions with a trained Christ-centered counselor or a close, trusted friend or pastor. Being anchored in the truth of God's love and grace is essential in working through insecurity. As God's love and grace for us become more real, we can acknowledge guilt and responsibility because our sense of value and worth is based on the permanence of His love and grace, and not on our inconsistent selves or others' inconsistent words or actions.

Our Creator made us as physical, spiritual, and emotional beings. Working through our painful emotions is a sign of maturity, and admitting fault or blame does not change your worth or value. It is acting in obedience to Christ and may even bring you closer to family members. While insecurity may be deeply rooted in our hearts, God gives us the answer we need for insecurity. His name is Jesus. When our physical, spiritual and emotional security is anchored in Christ, we no longer need to be faultless, accepted, or honored by others. Why? Because we have been declared faultless, accepted as we are, and lifted high by the King of Kings. All other opinions pale in comparison to His.

Insecurity and Worth

Reflection Questions:

1. When considering your life, where has your sense of security been found? In people's opinions? Performance? Wealth? Or something else?

2. Do you tend to take things personally or get offended easily? Why or why not?

3. Are you able to admit you are wrong and take responsibility, or do you typically blame-shift or justify your actions?

9

Managing Emotions

Texting your emotions through emojis is easy. Expressing your emotions well can be more difficult. Working through your emotions, i.e., acknowledging them or allowing yourself to feel and then express them is tough. We are complicated creatures. We are physical, mental, emotional, and spiritual beings. Every part of us interacts with every other part of us, and the result is us—a complicated mess. Our emotions alone are complicated as we may feel multiple emotions at the same time. The death of a loved one can bring about feelings of sadness, though we may be happy for them if they were a believer and we know they are in heaven. At the same time, we may fear moving forward without them and be angry because they are no longer here.

I've had numerous conversations with black-and-white thinkers who admit that emotions are often uncomfortable, unwelcome, complicated, and confusing. Depending on how you were raised, emotions may be more like an enemy. You avoid them, you kill them, or you stuff them deep down inside. They are neither welcomed nor something you work through. Because the all-or-nothing thinking is in control, difficult emotions are often pushed to the nothing category. Negative emotions such as hurt, pain, rejection, fear, loneliness, sadness and grief may at most be acknowledged but are never allowed to remain on the surface. Black-and-white thinkers typically don't like the nuances and abstractions of feelings as they are complicated and confusing. They will either choose to feel or not to feel, or perhaps simplify their life by overlooking the multiple emotions and funneling them into one emotion, such as anger. But if a black-and-white thinker wants to have healthy relationships, they must understand and express thier emotions in healthy ways. Why? Because healthy relationships require emotional connections such as compassion, empathy, love, and joy. And these emotional connections with others only come when one works through the difficult emotions themselves.

Black-and-white thinkers who were raised in relationally-detached homes express emotions differently than those raised in more affectionate homes. Individuals raised in affectionate homes with positive relationships seem to function in relationships better because they were allowed to express their feelings and encouraged to work out their feelings within relationships. Those who have been raised in relationally-detached homes with abusive or emotionally stunted relationships often distance themselves from most emotions and find it difficult to work through them well. Because of this struggle, they have difficulty sympathizing or empathizing with others, causing difficulties in relationships.

Sadness. Individuals who grew up in relationally-detached homes often view sadness as weak or foolish. You deal with it by "sucking it up" and moving on, not allowing yourself to grieve or feel sad. You cope with sadness by "pulling yourself up by the bootstraps." Any feelings of hurt or sadness may be forced below the surface and never dealt with, or they may be expressed only through anger. Black-and-white thinkers who were reared in affectionate homes, however, are typically allowed to express sadness and may receive support, though it may not be accepted. Since black-and-white thinking is typically all or nothing, black-and-white thinkers may push their sadness to the nothing side and refuse to feel it because it is uncomfortable.

Happiness. If a black-and-white thinker is raised in a relationally-detached home, they may be unlikely to find joy and happiness within relationships, though there still is a need for relationship. More typically, they find pleasure in performance-related activities such as excelling in academics, athletics, or at their place of employment. Therefore, hard work and success are often valued and feelings of pride in self-accomplishment equals happiness. This attitude often frustrates spouses who seek happiness through a relationship. Being raised in an affectionate home may help a black-and-white thinker recognize the importance of relationships and to value people more, which in turn, leads to happier relationships. Nothing in Scripture states that God wants us to be happy or that happiness should be our goal. Happiness is often a result of placing Him first in our lives and relationships.

Anger. Anger is easier to feel and express than hurt or rejection. It's simpler. You express it, let it out, and then you feel better—mostly. If you are a black-and-white thinker who grew up in a detached home, anger may have been the only emotion you observed and felt. In physically and emotionally abusive homes, anger is the ruling emotion, and it was likely expressed regularly. Some vow never to physically hit others like they were hit, but the inability to sort out and work through other emotions or recognize the importance of relationships continues to bring about a different kind of abuse. Emotional abuse.

In emotional abuse, anger continues to reign and expressing it is a way to control another person so they do what you want. Anger poorly expressed impacts the relationship profoundly. The spouse may begin to live in fear of the other person as their anger, intimidation, and control sets the relationship on a disconnected and downward spiral. For black-and-white thinkers who have been raised in affectionate families where abuse was nonexistent, anger exists, yet it often does not dominate. A person may feel angry when the situation is perceived as bad or wrong. Anger can be expressed in either unhealthy or healthy ways, but ignoring or not dealing with the anger is not an option. I have observed that most black-and-white thinkers from affectionate families are more likely to work out their anger within their relationships than those who have not been raised in such families. Individuals from affectionate upbringings are more likely to apologize and seek forgiveness for actions and expressed anger which helps relationships succeed.

As a relational thinker, I am tempted to respond to negative emotions in the same way a black-and-white thinker does. I prefer to ignore the negative emotions and hope they will go away. If black-and-white thinkers and relational thinkers are to mature emotionally and relationally and enjoy healthy relationships, emotions ought to be admitted, felt, processed, and worked through. For black-and-white thinkers raised in detached homes, this would most likely require the help of a trained counselor and a willingness to change. Most are not willing to change or do not recognize a need for change unless their relationship with a spouse is either at or past the breaking point. By then, it may be too late. It is not uncommon to see a spouse (typically a wife) leave her black-and-white thinker husband because of his emotional disconnection or abuse, only to find that when the relationship is threatened, the husband is seemingly willing to change. But the wife has already been too hurt and cannot trust her husband. Addressing these issues before it gets to the breaking point could save the marriage and allow for a better life and relationships. Though I have seen some extremely detached black-and-white thinker individuals change to the point of saving their marriages, it required humility, brokenness, the willingness to work through emotions, and the conviction of the Holy Spirit.

Some black-and-white thinkers are passionate individuals who allow their emotions to lead their reactions and responses. Previously it was stated how many black-and-white thinkers tend to lean toward the "nothing" in feeling emotions, yet other black-and-white thinkers tend to lean toward the "all" with their emotions. In other words, emotions may go from zero to sixty in less than three seconds, and the reaction may be very intense. This intensity may lead to extreme anger for some, but for others, it may lead to suicidal thoughts. Insecurities, past hurts, or heart demands may trigger such intense emotional reactions that others want to get far away. Learning how to control one's emotions and address the triggers are important steps to ensure the healthy expression of emotions. While the time from zero to sixty may be short, the desire to change, with the help of the Holy Spirit, helps pause the reaction. The need to change will make this pause a priority. Our emotions are important to recognize and feel, but they ought not control us or our relationships.

While this book is not a resource on how to handle emotions, here are a few tips to get started:

1. *Taming the Tongue* – Besides the numerous Proverbs that talk about the one who is quick to anger, James compares the tongue to a rudder that can steer a ship (Chap 3). Both good and bad can flow from the tongue, but when it is used to vent

our emotions, especially anger, it will steer any relationship off a proverbial cliff. Taming the tongue means that you make a decision to withhold any emotional reaction, be silent, and speak how and when it is wise to do so. This is also known as filtering. Some people speak their minds and lack the emotional consideration (i.e. filter) of how their words will affect others. Making a conscious decision that stems from your heart's desire to honor God and value others is wise. Ultimately, taming the tongue involves a heart change as "out of the heart the mouth speaks" (Lk 6:45). Self-control, or tongue-control, is a fruit of the Spirit (Gal 6) that takes place when your heart is submitting to His. Additionally, allow your love for others to trump your "need" to speak your mind. There may be some serious tongue-biting, but a love for others and consideration of how words will affect them will help give pause as to whether something should be said or not.

2. Take Frustration to the Lord – While it is foolish to vent our feelings and emotions whenever we feel them, we do need to process them. There is a time and a place, and certain people who we ought to process with and certain people we cannot, but we *can* process our emotions with the Lord. He hears all who come to Him, because He cares for you (1 Pet 5:7). Speaking out loud to Him when we're alone is better than speaking to Him in our heads. Hearing ourselves express our thoughts and emotions helps us to process, but it can also scare us. In the Psalms, David often voiced his frustrations and fears to God, but he eventually came to trust in Him. Taking the example from David's playbook, our prayer might sound like this: *"God. I am so frustrated! I don't know why they are against me, and they are driving me crazy. I'm hurt, frustrated, and I can't take much more. But you have placed them in my life and you are using them to conform me into your likeness. So help my heart to change so that I can love well and be a witness for you. I trust you as you are my Rock and my Hiding Place. My hope is in you alone."* Taming our tongue is a great start. Voicing our frustrations to God, while placing our trust in Him is equally, if not more important.

3. Discern What is in the Heart – Often we feel certain emotions because we perceive words or actions in certain ways. While we need to be humble about our perceptions, there may be desires in our hearts that may be ruling us. What is it you wanted? What did you need? What did you expect? Are your expectations realistic? Why is this important? Why are you having such a strong reaction? The stronger the reaction, the more significant it is in your heart. Jeremiah 17:9 states that the heart is "wicked" and "beyond cure" and "understanding." Our hearts have a propensity for evil and for self-centeredness. My wants, needs, and desires typically come before what others want and desire, and certainly come before God's wants and desires. We're the victims, we need to be in control, our happiness is important and should be to others, we do more than others, etc.—all of these reflect our heart's propensities. Yet God wants our hearts to reflect His. Do you want to honor God in your response? Is this about having your own way or about God's way? Have you surrendered your heart and will to His? We will not change if our hearts are not changed, and the only one who can change our hearts is Christ. If there is anything in the heart not of Christ, confess this to Him and repent of this. Ask Him to change your heart, yield your will to His, and over time, your heart will change.

4. Return to the Person – After you have completed these first three steps, and your desire is to honor God and the other person with your response, you are likely ready to approach the other person calmly. If the frustration returns, you may need to complete the first few steps again.

Stu was a passionate follower of Jesus Christ. His love for Jesus could be seen by others within only a few moments of meeting him or seeing him in action. He often turned conversations toward evangelizing and led many people to Christ throughout the years. His passion and zeal sometimes made others feel uncomfortable, including Christians. When confronted, he criticized them for lacking a passion for Christ. His family saw Stu's passion for Jesus, but they also were recipients of his anger. Stu became angry very quickly and blew up at his family when they did not meet his expectations or what he thought were God's expectations. He quoted the Bible and defended himself by stating that Christ can return any minute, so there is an urgency to preach and for the family to obey. He didn't care if he offended anyone because the gospel is offensive only to the unbeliever. He thought everyone should be as passionate for Christ as he was. Stu's passion for Jesus was a great example for many Christians, yet in his home life, his anger frightened his children and turned them away from God. They often called him a hypocrite behind his back, even though he recognized he sinned and frequently asked for their forgiveness.

Stu agreed to go to counseling with his wife and learned to control his immediate reaction. In those times, he made a rule not to react to bad behavior immediately and left the room, turning to God in prayer. He asked the Lord to search his heart and often found he was living by a religious law and trying to force his children to love God. He began to see his family through the lens of grace and chose to love them regardless of what they had done. He spoke to his children and taught them God's Word only when his emotions were in check and after prayer and discussions with his wife. Stu's emotions and passions often led him more than the Spirit, but He learned to control his emotions and follow the Spirit.

Being created in the image of God means that we will have a myriad of emotions. To deny our emotions is to deny the image of God in us. To allow our emotions to control us is to disallow the Spirit to work through us. Expressing our emotions in healthy ways demonstrates self-control and value for others in our lives. And when we value others' emotions through listening and responding in love and compassion, we reflect Christ more fully. May the God of all emotions give you the courage to feel, the strength to be silent when needed, and the love to express yourself in ways that value others and God above all else.

Reflection Questions:

1. Are you aware of your emotions on a regular basis? How do you express them and who do you express them to?

2. Which emotions do you feel most comfortable expressing? Which are the least comfortable?

3. Do you allow your emotions to be the engine in your reactions and responses or the caboose? In other words, do you allow your emotions to lead and control you, or do you control them?

10

The Heart of Anger

"You're always doing that!"

"You never (fill in the blank)!"

"That stupid, #@!*%!"

You probably don't have to look too far in the distant past to remember the last time you've been angry. Anger is a universal emotion. It is an emotional reaction to situations or circumstances that we find unfair, unjust, or simply wrong. Being created in God's image means that we will experience anger as He does, though admittedly, our anger is often tainted by our sin and is not righteous like His. Throughout the Old Testament, God's anger and wrath are poured out on humanity for sins against Him and others. In the New Testament, God turns His judgment on His Son for our sins.

Several themes of anger are consistent with black-and-white thinking. These include (1) being right vs. being wrong or the need to meet a standard, and (2) difficulty of reconciliation.

Being Right vs. Being Wrong

Two factors generally contribute to the black-and-white thinker's anger: what is right, and the need to be right.

First, anger typically occurs when something happens that we know is not right. Since we are created in God's image, we essentially are created to become angry at what is wrong. If you learn of sexual or physical abuse to children, do you become angry at the perpetrator? Of course you do. It is how we are made. Ultimately, we ought to be angry at sin and evil and at all the things with which God is angry. But since sin entered the world, our anger has not been aligned with God's anger. Instead of being angry at sin, we are prone to welcome sin into our lives. The focus of our anger then shifts from being angry at the breaking of God's law to the breaking of our own laws.

We don't need to look much further for an illustration of anger than the biblical account of Jonah. After first running from God, Jonah finally relented and went to Nineveh. He delivered his message of repentance and waited. He wanted God to wipe the Ninevites off the face of the earth. To Jonah's chagrin, they believed his message and turned from their sinful ways, Therefore God spared them the wrath that their sins deserved. When God didn't give the Ninevites any punishment, but mercy instead,

Jonah became so angry he wished to die. Jonah was angry at God because God did not meet Jonah's expectations. God *should* have wiped them out because it's what they deserved, but He didn't.

Our anger is not much different than Jonah's. We get angry at ourselves because we did not meet our own standards. We get angry with others because they did not meet our expectations. We get angry at God because He did not respond the way we think He should have. Remember, when we either say or hear the word *should* in a sentence, we ought to be alerted that there is a standard or expectation presented. The day I wrote this, I became angry at a driver at my sons' school for parking in the student drop-off lane. Why? Because that's the student drop-off lane – not the parking lane. That's the rule! And he was breaking it, causing a multiple-vehicle backup because he didn't follow the rules. He should have known better! He should have been more considerate of others! You get the idea.

So, our anger has shifted from God's law being broken to our standards not being met. When that happens, others deserve our wrath or correction. We may have a right way to do something and we'll tell others to do things our way. How many conflicts occur because people are not doing things the right way, like emptying the dishwasher, cleaning the room, or driving a car? When such "correction" occurs, the other person often feels they can't do anything right and may see you as being controlling, because that's what is happening.

Or perhaps these laws are not our laws, per se, but societal laws or even unwritten laws. Most of us have experienced merging into one lane before construction on a highway. When merging to the left lane, many people say you should get over to the left lane as soon as possible and wait in line. Often a truck or car will block the right lane because the unwritten law says it's unfair to pass everyone else while they wait in line. I've learned that we're supposed to use both lanes and merge at the merge point, but people feel it's wrong and block the lane. In anger, we feel justified because others did wrong according to the laws, and since we believe we are in the right, they are all "idiots." And when we're angry, we're always in the right, even though we're often wrong.

The second factor that triggers right vs. wrong anger deals with pride. When pride enters the picture, which it does for all of us, the need to be right in our own eyes and the eyes of others often gains momentum. Some black-and-white thinkers feel the need to be right and find their esteem in being right. When being right becomes more important than anything else, anger is often used to keep others quiet to maintain the illusion that they are right. Anger, then, is used more as a control tactic to silence others and remain in the right—often while being wrong. Criticisms +

correction = controlling behaviors. Add pride and anger to the mix, and this is likely to equal abuse.

Difficulty with Reconciliation

Many black-and-white thinkers struggle with reconciliation. When there is a deep hurt in a relationship, many black-and-white thinkers will choose to deal with it by not dealing with it. Some will completely cut off the relationship, while others will emotionally disconnect by simply doing their duty without desiring anything more. Anger, however, is better resolved through a process of reconciliation. Reconciliation is more likely to occur when the one who has wronged the other acknowledges their wrongdoing, seeks forgiveness (Mt 5:24) and then demonstrates a change in behavior that comes from brokenness (Mt 3:8). Reconciliation also occurs when forgiveness is granted (Mt 18:22) and both parties are willing to move forward in the relationship and work on trust. Granting forgiveness for past hurts may be difficult for some black-and-white thinkers since forgiveness is not a concrete concept. Granting forgiveness may be difficult because it goes against a works-related attitude of "you get what you deserve." Forgiveness requires grace, or the "giving what you don't deserve" attitude. It is taking the undeserved sin or debt upon themselves, and letting the offender, who hasn't earned it, off the hook. Forgiveness can never be earned but is freely given and is not for the offender but for God and us! Just as we will never deserve God's forgiveness, others will not deserve ours. But as we forgive as God has forgiven us, we are released from our anger and freed from resentment. Many black-and-white thinkers' form of forgiveness is to simply not think about the offense or bring it up anymore. While this may contain some aspects of forgiveness, it falls short of actual reconciliation, which involves working through the emotions of hurt, brokenness, and love. When we fail to work through these emotions, anger can remain the dominant emotion.

Is acknowledging the wrong and apologizing enough to reconcile and move forward? For some, yes, because apologizing is a tangible action and the wrongdoer may take corrective measures to show they've changed. Some may not find a need to apologize, but simply to recognize where they may have been "mistaken," correct the mistake, and move forward. This seems more like taking responsibility for actions without admitting fault. It falls short, however, of taking responsibility for the relationship or complete reconciliation.

Some black-and-white thinkers don't recognize that apologies help heal brokenness that exists in the relationship. Some more severe black-and-white thinkers have an extremely hard time even being broken over their sin as they cannot empathize with those they hurt. They have not felt these emotions themselves for a long time because they are uncomfortable, painful or too difficult to grasp.

Some additional reasons for anger in the black-and-white thinker include situations perceived as being unfair, anger masking depression, or anger used as a defense mechanism to protect oneself against hurt. Self-protection against being hurt is learned early in life, and some say causes black-and-white thinking. Though I won't say it is a cause, it can certainly be a heavy influence leading to stronger black-and-white thinking and weaker relational thinking.

If you see this thinking in your anger, begin by looking at your own heart. Realize that you have not met God's expectations either and are deserving of the same anger you have toward others. But in His love and grace, God poured His anger on His Son instead of you. Acknowledge that other people may be wrong, but you have also been wrong—many times. Thank God for His undeserved grace and love. Instead of casting you and I aside and removing us from His presence, He chooses to reconcile us to Himself through Christ. When he received the punishment we deserved, we were on his heart and mind. Let Christ's love for you be the catalyst for reconciliation.

Reflection Questions:

1. When does black-and-white thinking happen in your anger? What rules are being broken? What expectations do you have?

2. How will God's unmerited favor toward you, an undeserving person, influence your response toward others who are undeserving?

3. In what areas can you improve with reconciliation? Do you humble yourself to admit you are wrong? Have you forgiven those who sinned against you? Do you ask for forgiveness and set your mind to change for the relationship?

11

Black-and-White Thinking in Anxiety

Most of us have experienced anxiety at some time. We worry about our children, our jobs, or our schooling. We feel anxious when we have an interview, have to speak or sing in public, or attend some unfamiliar event or activity that pulls us out of our comfort zone.

When my wife and I were dating, I told her I would propose to her after she received the twelfth rose from me. For about two months, I gave her one or two roses at a time. Finally, I was approaching the twelfth rose. While dining at a restaurant, I excused myself to "go to the restroom." I then went to retrieve the final roses from the trunk of my car and walked back into the restaurant. With sweaty palms, a heart beating so loud I was certain others could hear, and a stomach churning with anticipation, I asked for her hand in marriage. Why I was so anxious then, I have no idea. I knew she would accept my proposal, yet my anxiety level was high—probably because this was the biggest decision of my life—and one of the best.

Anxiety occurs because we are fearful. The greater the fear, the greater the anxiety. If we are only slightly afraid of spiders, we will avoid them or get others to kill them. If we are deathly afraid of them, we will probably freak out. Most of us either push ourselves through fearful situations through courage, prayer, or support from others, or we avoid them.

When anxiety disrupts everyday life, it is considered a disorder. Extreme anxiety may lead to compulsions or actions to ease the fears. The fear is an itch that must be scratched, and the compulsion is the scratch. Many struggle with a serious anxiety disorder known as Obsessive Compulsive Disorder (OCD). OCD involves specific fears that reign in the heart and ruminate in the mind. The struggler believes the only way to quell the fear is to obey the compulsion. A fear of germs, sickness, and death will lead to continuous hand washing. A fear of death by someone breaking in will lead to unlocking and locking the door numerous times to be certain the door is locked. If a person with OCD cannot complete these ritualistic compulsions, their anxiety will increase.

Black-and-white thinking is evident in several ways with anxiety. First, black-and-white thinking occurs when the level of fear goes quickly past "slightly afraid" to "mostly/all afraid." The fear becomes so intense that there is only one way to end it—compulsion. The person has to be all afraid or not afraid. Completing a compulsive ritual signifies that the act is either handled perfectly or incorrectly. An individual with OCD who is fearful of germs, and subsequently sickness or death, is compelled to wash in a way they know will quell the fear for the time being.

If they do it the wrong way, the fear intensifies. There is no settling or 'good enough' mentality when dealing with fear. One cannot simply wash their hands once. The person with OCD must do it in a certain way the exact number of times to be right and for it to work.

Black-and-white thinking is also prevalent in perfectionists. Perfectionists often struggle with anxiety or depression because their standards are so high. That's the *all* in the "all or nothing." They must achieve a certain standard; to do less or perform poorly is to fail. Many black-and-white thinkers will work extremely hard to measure up to their standards. The standards are so high that it produces anxiety just trying to meet them—as if a ruthless dictator set the standards and threatens their life. Panic, fear, and stress prevail. The perfectionist is enslaved to an insatiable tyrant who holds on to a strict law that must be obeyed, or a standard that must be met. Freedom will only come when the law of grace begins to penetrate the law of works in your heart and mind (see Chap 4).

Andy is a perfectionist. Growing up in a poor home, Andy determined in high school he would never become like his parents. Andy worked diligently in school to get straight A's and joined Student Government and other clubs to be attractive to Ivy League colleges. After entering college, he declared a double major in Pre-Med and Applied Mathematics. Andy struggled with his classes and often became both depressed and anxious because of his grades and the pressure he put on himself. His goals and his perfectionism led him to a breakdown and hospitalization. His perfectionism even leaked into his relationship with his girlfriend, but when his girlfriend became tired of being criticized, she dumped him, causing more emotional distress. Andy needed counseling help, but he refused to lower the expectations on himself and eventually found his way into another breakdown.

In addition to having high standards for themselves, perfectionists also have high standards for others. If the perfectionist sets high standards for others, that person will likely experience anxiety while trying to make the black-and-white perfectionist happy. They often feel oppressed under the watchful eye of the perfectionist. While perfectionism may work better at a place of employment, it has a detrimental effect in closer relationships. Holding family members to high standards, especially in the little things, has been known to cause many conflicts in relationships. While there certainly are standards that ought to be met, such as telling the truth, being responsible, and respecting others, correcting others ought to be handled relationally, rather than in anger or as a law enforcer. Left unaddressed, the anxiety levels of others will remain high. If anxiety levels are high, the family members will often do what they can to avoid being in your presence. If avoidance follows anxiety, children will choose to spend more time away from home, and separation or divorce from a spouse is likely to occur.

Not only is black-and-white thinking found in perfectionism and OCD, but it may also occur with everyday worries and anxieties. When we worry, we often think about worst-case scenarios. "Something bad happened to them!" "They could be laying on the side of the road, dead!" "I'm going to look like a fool!" "I'm going to fail!" "I'll be rejected!" Dwelling on worst-case scenarios is in itself black-and-white thinking. Worriers reason that if they think of the worst thing that can happen at least they will be prepared for it. But they've also lost time, energy, and rest in the present while predicting an unlikely outcome.

Recognizing that black-and-white thinking is present in anxiety is important so that we see our involvement in our anxieties. Anxiety is not simply something that happens to you, but something that can be addressed. If we know we are actively involved in our worries, we can also be actively involved in our healing. When we feel anxious, we can note our thoughts and begin to exchange them with the truth. I encourage clients to write their fears in a notebook, followed by copying Scripture verses that address the fear. For example, if someone has anxiety about financial struggles, they can write down and memorize Genesis 50:21. "Now therefore, do not be afraid. I will provide for and support you and your little ones. And he comforted them and spoke to their hearts."

Not only must our thoughts change, but also our hearts. As we experience anxious thoughts, it's important to recognize that anxiety is fear, and God speaks to our fears. Replacing our black-and-white thoughts with the truths of God as found in Scripture and believing them will be important for change.

If you completed a Scripture word search for the words "Fear not" or "Do not be afraid," you would find a promise either before or after most of them. "Fear not, for I am with you" (Isa 41:10). "Fear not. I have redeemed you. I have called you by name" (Isa 43:1). "Do not be afraid ... for the Lord your God will be with you" (Josh 1:9). "The Lord Himself will go before you and will be with you. Do not be afraid" (Duet 31:8). It is in these promises of His presence and faithfulness to us that we are to take comfort because they come from a God who is love and who speaks to us when we are anxious. They come from a God who will never leave us nor forsake us. They come from a God who promises that "all things work together for the good of those who love Him; who are called according to His purpose" (Rom 8:28).

Growing in grace continues to be the answer for those who struggle with black-and-white thinking. Grace frees us from the tyranny of perfectionism, encourages us when standards are not met, and empowers us to become more like Him. Applying grace to our anxieties helps us to overcome OCD and other anxieties as we draw nearer to Him. As we grow in grace and knowledge of Him, he gradually changes us, reduces our anxieties, and gives us peace.

Reflection Questions:

1. List some of your greatest fears on the left side of a blank sheet of paper. What does God's Word say about your fears? Write these verses down across from your fears and refer back to this paper when you struggle with anxiety.

2. How are you actively involved in your anxieties? Do your anxieties lead you to compulsive or controlling behaviors? If so, what are they? Confess them and seek His peace.

3. How can applying God's grace to your anxieties help you in your struggle? Ask God to help you to grow in your understanding of grace.

12

Black-and-White Thinking in Depression

According to the Mayo Clinic, depression is "a mood disorder that causes a persistent feeling of sadness and loss of interest."[4] It is characterized by low energy or fatigue, change in appetite and sleep, low self-esteem, poor concentration or inability to make decisions, and feelings of hopelessness. Feelings of numbness, guilt, shame, and being unloved can be oppressive and lead to inactivity and loneliness. The more severe the depression, the more likely the oppression controls your thoughts, actions, and mood, which means the more powerless you feel to control yourself.

Whether depression itself causes negative thought patterns or these thought patterns cause depression, I can say with certainty that they are present in depression. Changing thought patterns are known to be helpful in combatting depression, and one of the most common thought patterns found in depression is black-and-white thinking.

Black-and-white thinking occurs in depression in both interpretation and declarations. Interpretations include how we interpret situations and words, and declarations are what we believe and state is true. When black-and-white thinkers hear certain words or confront some situations, they often interpret them as all or nothing. For example, a student who is depressed will tell herself after receiving a B on a test, "I failed it. I'm stupid." A father who did not handle a situation well will tell himself, "I'm a lousy father. I'm a failure." If they meet a high standard, then it is *all good*. If they don't, it is *all bad*. In these examples, *all bad* means failing and therefore results in self-punishment by calling oneself a failure or stupid.

People struggling with depression draw similar conclusions about themselves. "You don't love me." "No one cares." "I am a failure." "All is hopeless." "Nothing will help me." "I tried everything. Nothing works." Depression worsens when the person thinks in black-and-white and then believes their own conclusions. They subsequently declare these beliefs to be true. I believe no one cares, so it is therefore true – no one cares. If the depressed person believes what they think about themselves and continues in these beliefs, even if they are not accurate, the depression will deepen.

The perfectionistic thinking that is prevalent in those struggling with anxiety is also present in those who are depressed. In the previous examples, we know a letter grade of B is certainly not failing. Far from it. The father may not have handled a situation well, but that does not mean that he is a horrible father. He likely does many things well. In black-and-white thinking, the simple conclusion is that it has to be one or the other. To conclude that a B is not a failure or that a good father can make poor decisions at times is difficult for a depressed person to comprehend, let alone believe. While most people will agree that "nobody's perfect," many black-and-white thinkers will remain perfectionists and struggle with being satisfied in relationships or situations.

All of us are both sufferers and participants. Sufferers of depression not only feel oppressed by the depression, but they also participate in the depression. They actively or passively engage in the depression by thinking depressive thoughts, believing these thoughts, wearing dark clothes, remaining in bed, living with high expectations, or following one's feelings. It may not seem as though there is a choice in these matters, but that is only how it feels, not necessarily what is true.

To combat black-and-white thinking in depression or depression in general, we need to reach new conclusions based on different truths. These new truths ought to be based not on our flawed interpretations, but on God's Word. Introducing the themes of God's truth and grace into our depressive thinking challenges any black-and-white thinking.

And what are these new conclusions based on God's truth? Let's go back to the examples of the B grade and the failing father. In both cases, the truth of God's Word (based on Rom 2:8, 3:23, 8:1; Jn 3:16) is the following: "I may not have done as well as I would have liked, or maybe even failed, yet I can expect to do poorly at times as 'All have sinned and fall short.' But who I am is based on Christ's actions for me, not mine. Therefore, I may have failed, but I am not a failure. I am loved, worthwhile, blessed, cherished, and adored by Him, not because of what I have or have not done, but because of who He is."

Others may benefit from these truths: "I know I failed or did poorly. My failures were taken to the cross by Jesus. Therefore, I do not need to punish myself any further by calling myself names or dwelling on my failings, as my punishment fell on Christ." When these truths become more important than personal truths and conclusions, and when the depressed person believes them more than their truths, they can find relief from their depression.

It all sounds simple enough, yet it is difficult for someone who is depressed to think differently because they have been thinking negatively for a long time. At times, supplements or medication may be necessary to help change their thinking. Other times, no medication is necessary; only someone to minister to the depressed person and repeat God's truths to challenge their black-and-white thinking.

Shame

Those who are depressed often feel shame. While shame is often found in the same sentence as guilt, they are very different. Guilt is feeling bad about failing. Shame is taking it a step further into a personal attack. It's not simply that I failed, but *I* am a failure. It's not just doing something that is bad, but *I* am bad. The difference between the two is the personal nature that arises and is adopted by the person. In other words, the actions one did or didn't do become the identity of the person. In situations of abuse, the actions that another did often result in the victim feeling shame as well. In all these situations, actions become identity. Accepting this identity often leads to depression.

Self-worth and identity are often at the crux of depression. When self-worth is based on our own actions or another's actions toward us, we often find ourselves on shifting sand. When we are successful, we feel good about ourselves. When we fail, we may feel down or angry at ourselves. When others say good or bad things, we feel up or down. When we accept or believe their words or believe our own thoughts about ourselves, which is often based on our actions, then our self-worth and identity will fluctuate.

In Matthew 7, Jesus speaks about the wise and foolish builders (24–29). He states the wise builders are those who both hear his words and put them into practice. The wise builder's house was built on a solid rock which withstood the rains, winds, and floods. The foolish builders, on the other hand, heard the words, but did not apply them to their lives. Their house was built on sand and collapsed with the rains, winds, and floods. Similarly, those who hear God's words and accept His love and grace have an identity and worth that is built on the Rock and the truth of God's Word.

Their identity is not formed by their failings or another's words or actions, but by God's unmerited favor. In other words, it's based on Christ's performance on the cross, not our performance here. Nor is it based on what we or others say about ourselves, but about what God says. Romans 5:8 states, "God shows his love for us in that while we were still sinners, Christ died for us." Those who hear the truth but don't apply such truths to their lives will have lives built on shifting sand. When difficult situations arise, their worlds collapse because they did not apply God's truth to their lives. Building our lives on the Rock (Jesus) means we accept and believe His truth. His actions define us, not our own. When we believe these truths, our guilt and shame are taken with Christ onto the cross, and his righteousness falls on us. Do you believe you are righteous through Christ?

Francine's mother verbally abused her. She called Francine names and told her she would not amount to anything. Francine's father left when she was two years old and had not been heard from since. As she matured, she looked for love and positive attention from others, especially men. She was taken advantage of by many guys she met, including the man she married. Despite his faults, he was a decent man who recently came to know Christ personally. He gradually became less self-centered and showered her with praise for all she had done for the family. While Francine appreciated his words, she never believed him and frequently felt like she could never measure up. She would acknowledge that she was a Christian, but the joy Christians feel always alluded her. She knew it was because of all the bad things she did when she was younger. Her past sexual life, her abortions, and her frequent failings as a mother and wife just piled on top of the abuse she felt as a child. After years of self-condemnation and shame, she decided to go to counseling after she scared herself with thoughts of suicide. After hearing her life story, her therapist talked to her about grace and God's love. Francine knew these truths in her head, but these truths never entered her heart. She did not believe them to be true. Through counseling, journaling, small groups, and meeting with a mentor, Francine began to accept God's truth. When thoughts of shame and failure crept into her mind, she challenged them. She began to see herself as God sees her through Christ, and not as she saw herself through her past performance. She was no longer enslaved by shame as a failure, but through Christ she became free as a daughter of the King. She repeated her favorite verse to herself, Romans 8:1, "Therefore there is now no condemnation for those who are in Christ Jesus."

Suicidal Thinking

I was twelve years of age when the first thoughts of suicide crept into my mind. I moved to a new house, started a new school and didn't have a lot of friends. I was overweight, girls weren't attracted to me, and I felt awfully alone. I remember thinking, with a knife to my chest, "If this is how life is going to be, I don't want to live anymore." Without the support and encouragement of my sister and one or two friends, I do not know if I would have made it through this dark time.

Can you hear the black-and-white, all or nothing thinking that was evident in my words, "If this is how life is going to be, I don't want to live anymore"? I did not see this time simply as a difficult time, it was all or nothing. Either life has to be great, or life should end.

Many who consider suicide possess black-and-white-thinking. There are often two choices in their minds: 1) either live a life of suffering that won't get better, or 2) commit suicide. In their minds, life will not get better. Perhaps this conclusion has been drawn because life has been difficult and unbearable up to this point. It is difficult to see anything beyond this present darkness, but additional darkness. If this is you, you are not alone. Our past does not determine our future, and present pain does not predict future realities. The jailor in the book of Acts 16 experienced this firsthand.

"About midnight Paul and Silas were praying and singing hymns to God, and the other prisoners were listening to them. Suddenly there was such a violent earthquake that the foundations of the prison were shaken. At once all the prison doors flew open, and everyone's chains came loose. The jailer woke up, and when he saw the prison doors open, he drew his sword and was about to kill himself because he thought the prisoners had escaped. But Paul shouted, 'Don't harm yourself! We are all here!'

The jailer called for lights, rushed in and fell trembling before Paul and Silas. He then brought them out and asked, 'Sirs, what must I do to be saved?'

They replied, 'Believe in the Lord Jesus, and you will be saved—you and your household.' Then they spoke the word of the Lord to him and to all the others in his house. At that hour of the night the jailer took them and washed their wounds; then immediately he and all his household were baptized. The jailer brought them into his house and set a meal before them; he was filled with joy because he had come to believe in God—he and his whole household" (25-33).

The jailor was asleep on the job. Perhaps the singing of the prisoners wooed him to sleep. However, when the earthquake hit and he awoke to see the prison doors open, he was about to kill himself because he thought the prisoners escaped. He could not see into the actual cells, but based on what he could see, he assumed they had escaped and therefore, he and his whole family would be punished for his mistakes. He predicted a future reality based on the present circumstance. It wasn't until he heard a voice crying out from the darkness that alerted him to a different reality. "Don't harm yourself, we are all here!" It was only when he listened to the voice, and brought light into the present circumstances that he could understand there were more than two options. It wasn't a) suffering or b) suicide. With the shout of a voice and light in his circumstance, a third option presented itself.

He chose the third option, and he and his whole household were saved.

Those who think suicidal thoughts need to be shown there are more than two options, more than the black-and-white options that are presented. While life can be difficult at times, and sometimes for long periods of time, our present and past circumstances do not guarantee our future realities. There is hope that is found when we listen to that voice and we allow God's light to reveal to us what we need to know to get through difficult times. If you are suicidal, I encourage you to hang on to the hope of the gospel, talk to a counselor, and call the suicide prevention hotline at 1-800-273-8255 if you are in a crisis.

A single chapter on depression is hardly enough to do justice on the intricacies of such a complex struggle. Battling depression involves more than changing thought patterns and beliefs, both of which are important. It will also involve addressing actions, body and brain chemistry, and diet and exercise. My goal is only to highlight how black-and-white thinking is common in depression and summarize a few truths one might find helpful. If this is an issue you struggle through, I would encourage you to seek additional help and read Ed Welch's book, *Depression: A Stubborn Darkness*[8]. His insights would prove helpful for anyone struggling with depression or for those who love those with depression.

Reflection Questions

1. What goes through your mind when you are feeling down or depressed? How about others you love?

2. What typically wins in your struggles, the guilt or shame of falling short of standards, or the grace of God given through Christ's meeting of the standards?

3. Do you struggle with believing the truth that God's love for you is not based on your failings, but on Christ's success on the cross?

13

The Black-and-White Thinking Leader

Leaders come in all shapes, sizes, and personalities. Think back through all the leaders you've been under—pastors, managers or CEOs, even your teachers. You'll find strengths and weaknesses in all of them. Some you liked. Some you would like to forget. Some were more personable and caring, while others were more concerned with production and processes. Which type of leader did you respect the most? Enjoy the most? Which type was most effective as a leader?

Black-and-white thinking leaders typically value processes and production over the individual concerns of those they lead. That's not to say they don't appreciate people, but they are apt to value others more for what they do rather than who they are. Often, leaders who see things this way appraise people for what they produce and how well they meet standards. They may ignore or dismiss others' personal feelings and concerns, while workers who produce more are valued and respected to a greater degree. If the standards of production or attendance are subpar, the black-and-white thinker views workers as doing the wrong thing or failing. They may dismiss them altogether.

I recall that my fourth-grade teacher greatly valued hard work, responsibility, and follow-through. Although I did my homework regularly, I sometimes forgot it at home. After a few times, she became annoyed and took to calling me Forgetful Fred. A frown and a shake of the head showed her disappointment. She valued completed and turned in work over any hurt feelings.

My sixth-grade teacher was the opposite, and for obvious reasons, my favorite. Mrs. Crumb was a relational leader. She chose to encourage and show that she valued the person more than what they produced. She didn't ignore my grades or the quality of my work, but she also cared about me as a person. When students didn't perform well, she set out to encourage that person and get to know them better. They often improved because she showed she cared more about them than what they did. To put it succinctly, black-and-white thinking leaders value the product over the person, while relational-thinking leaders typically value the person over the product.

As parents who lead our children, the different parenting styles and values will reflect either black-and-white or relational tendencies. The parent who focuses on behaviors, correction, responsibility, obedience, meeting standards of performance in school, chores, or other work is the black-and-white thinker. The parent who is more sensitive to the emotions of the child, who provides comfort and focuses on the child's mental health and worth is the relational thinker. The former is typically stricter,

115

while the latter is often more lenient. Both have their place in parenting and are equally important, which is why parenting in a nuclear family is a co-leader responsibility and ideally not left to one person. Balancing both sides in a home, whether with two parents or living in a single parent home is important when leading the family.

Black-and-white thinking leaders have admirable strengths. They are called to accomplish the mission or produce what is set out in the vision. Since the black-and-white thinker focuses on the tangible, they are often driven to achieve success and to measure it accordingly. If you produce items, you measure success by the number of items produced or volume of sales. If the goal is to grow a larger church, success is calculated in numbers and giving. Although many would rightfully say church growth is measured in spiritual maturity, we can't ignore the numbers. If the goal is to teach students, we measure outcomes—grades, skill sets. Setting goals and deadlines and enlisting a leader who can reach them is good practice. Black-and-white thinking leaders are typically good at achieving goals, although they ought to be careful not to step on people's toes and feelings in the process.

Black-and-white thinking leaders are also concerned with the processes. Any process must be carried out in the right way, whichever is better, more efficient, traditional, or produces the best results in their mind. If it's not done the right way as they perceive it, it is wrong and therefore must be considered wrong, unbiblical, or unethical.

Matthew 18 defines a process for resolving conflict among believers. The party who was hurt is to go first to the offender. If they cannot resolve their differences, the offended is to bring a witness, and if the disagreement persists, to bring the matter to the church. For the black-and-white thinker, following this process is paramount. If a step is skipped or out of order, the whole process is flawed in the eyes of a black-and-white thinker.

In reality, conflict resolution gets messy, and it is not always as easy as following the Matthew 18 steps. If the process does not adhere to the letter of the law, then the black-and-white thinking leader may become upset because the biblical process was not followed correctly. To some black-and-white thinking pastors, the issue can become the process, and the actual concern or conflict becomes secondary. Sometimes, the first issue is never resolved because the black-and-white thinking pastor may be so stuck on doing things the right way that they are not able or willing to address the actual wrong.

This is what happened at a friend's church. Several couples approached the pastor at separate times complaining that he had been insensitive and lacked compassion for them during their marriage struggles. In these conversations, these couples felt their concerns were dismissed so they decided to leave the church, but maintained membership for the time. Through friendships, the leadership team learned of the experiences of these couples and approached the pastor. Since the pastor did not believe the process of Matthew 18 was followed through, the issue became about the couples' disobedience to the Word. The church voted to remove these couples from membership for refusing to follow the Word and being divisive. This caused a lot of pain for many congregants, leading several families to leave the church because of how it was handled.

Within an organization, the black-and-white thinking leader will see the written processes as being the right way, and any deviation as needing correction. Organizations love these types of leaders because they will reduce lawsuits or workplace accidents, thus saving the organization money and curtailing accidents. However, if the focus is only on the correct process, there may not be room to create new and better processes. People who hold to rigid ways of doing things will insist the old way is the way things should be done. If these situations are not handled well, friction erupts or grows between the black-and-white thinking leader and other leaders and employees.

Organizations will often develop the personality of their leader, creating a culture that may be more black-and-white, relational, or a balance of both. Some organizations, such as the military, police, and fire stations, have more of a black-and-white thinking culture due to the importance of following the processes and procedures for the sake of safety and clear lines of authority.

Without this culture, it is more than likely that lives would be lost and any discipline would be severely lacking. There are also churches who reflect a black-and-white thinking culture who can tend to become more legalistic and lack compassion and grace for those who do not measure up to certain standards. Based on his actions and words towards the Pharisees, I do not think Jesus had a 'law and behavior-focused' bride in his mind when he taught, healed, or demonstrated his love to others. But I do believe he wants his church to shed the things of this world for him.

In summary, families, organizations, and institutions all need black-and-white thinking leaders, pastors, and teachers to meet goals and achieve success. Many succeed in business, the classroom, and the pastorate. However, the more extreme one is in their black-and-white thinking, and the more pride that is present, the less relational they are. As a result, family members, employees, students, or church members may be hurt while under the tutelage of such a leader. The most successful and well-liked black-and-white thinking leaders are those who demonstrate the relational skills of compassion, empathy, mercy, and grace.

Reflection Questions

1. Who were your favorite teachers, bosses, or pastors? What traits did they have in common? Were they black-and-white thinkers or more relational thinkers?

2. Who were your least favorite teachers, bosses, or pastors? What traits did they possess that did not work for you? Were they black-and-white thinkers or more relational thinkers?

3. Considering the information in this chapter, what are your strengths as a leader? What do you still need to work on?

14

Black-and-White Thinking: A Mental Illness?

In their purest forms, both black-and-white and relational thinking reflect God the Father. As our creator and creator of the world, God the Father defines right and wrong, good and bad, and light and dark. He is the One who determines what is holy and what is not. He judges the actions and motives of humanity based on what is right. Moreover, God is the One who stands on truth because He is Truth. God is also relational, as we see throughout His interactions with us and with His Son whom He sent to reconcile us to Himself. If black-and-white thinking can reflect God, can we call it a mental illness?

If you were to Google the term "black-and-white thinking," most of the articles would show the worst parts of what many call a cognitive disorder, and would lead you to think that maybe you have Borderline Personality Disorder, Dissociative Identity Disorder, or are narcissistic. So perhaps now is a good time to differentiate between black-and-white thinking and mental illness.

Many, if not all of us, engage in black-and-white thinking in different aspects and times in our lives. Most of us have areas in our lives which we see as right or wrong, good or bad, either-or.

121

For example, many would argue there is a right and wrong way to eat an Oreo, put utensils in the dishwasher or toilet paper on the dispenser. We make moral judgments about actions and people (including ourselves) that are important to us. An example of an area where we may see things in black and white is politics, which of course, is aided by the current atmosphere of polarization. We may see only the extremes of the spectrum and believe that if you're not a Conservative Republican, you must be a Liberal Democrat. We seem to think there are only two options. However, we may not apply such thinking to all areas of our lives. Usually, as people mature and are involved in relationships some of the black-and-white thinking begins to erode, and relationships function better.

The National Alliance on Mental Illness (NAMI) defines a mental illness/disorder as "a condition that affects a person's thinking, feeling or mood."[5] Black-and-white thinking, also called *splitting* and *dichotomous thinking*, would be considered part of a mental disorder if it is a pattern that causes suffering or reduces a person's ability to function. If a person's black-and-white thinking negatively affects their success in their personal or professional relationships, most psychiatrists or psychologists would consider this extremely harmful. I agree. Black-and-white thinking is not listed as a mental disorder or illness, yet we frequently see this type of thinking in mental illnesses such as borderline personality disorder, narcissism, depression, and anxiety. Black-and-white thinking is also found in those struggling with afflictions such as Autism Spectrum Disorders. I think it is fair to conclude that black-and-white thinking is not a mental illness, but it is common in mental illnesses or disorders. We can also reason that not all people who think in black-and-white have a mental illness. In fact, most of us have areas in our lives where we think more in black-and-white. The determining factor is whether, and to what extent, it affects everyday relationships and employment. For this reason, it is important to address this type of thinking and for Christians to do so biblically.

Additionally, I would argue that God thinks in black-and-white. As previously stated, He is all-or-nothing, declares right from wrong, and wants us to be all in for Him, not lukewarm. While He is perfect and our thinking is tainted, there are many who reflect this part of Him more than the relational side, and others who reflect Him more relationally than in black-and-white thinking. Sin's enslavement—pride and the impact of childhood traumas—influence this thinking toward a mental health diagnosis.

Black-and-white thinking can often be used to simplify choices into an either-or, often because the abstract nature of the gray area can be too complicated. Determining something as right or wrong filters out the emotional middle ground, justifications and nuances that require additional thought, which are difficult for some people to grasp. This type of thinking may also be a defense mechanism for some, used to protect themselves from any negative comments so they may view themselves as being right and having worth.

Although we do not find the terms *mental illness* or *mental disorder* in Scripture, that does not mean that the Scriptures are silent or cannot speak to those diagnosed with mental illnesses. Nor does it imply that only psychotherapy can speak into mental health issues. The Bible is relevant for all our struggles and suffering—for relational and black-and-white thinkers alike.

Reflection Questions

1. What areas in your life do you engage in black-and-white thinking the most? How does the sinful nature affect your black-and-white thinking?

2. How do the Scriptures speak to you most in your struggles? What verses give you the most strength? Comfort? Hope?

15

Becoming Like Christ

If you're a black-and-white thinker, chances are you may be saying, "Give me something to do. I understand I need to change a few things, so how do I change or become more relational?" I'm so glad you asked that question because that is the purpose of this chapter.

The goal of the black-and-white thinker is not to become more like a relational thinker, but to become more like Christ. If you reflect God as a black-and-white thinker, then that is how you process or perceive situations and events. There is nothing to be ashamed of because there is nothing inherently wrong with processing through a black-and-white thinker's lens. Yet, as believers, we are encouraged by God to grow and mature (Heb 5:12). We are called to become more like Christ (Rom 8:29, 2 Cor 3:18, 1 Jn 3:2).

Becoming like Christ is no small task, but is a lifelong commitment and journey completed only when we are with Him for eternity (1 Jn 3:2). The process of becoming like Christ is a moment-by-moment, day-by-day process beginning with a heart of humility and leading to multiple God-honoring decisions and actions. While we wage a battle against the selfish desires of the flesh, we have a Wonderful Counselor, the Holy Spirit, who guides and empowers us as we cooperate with Him. It is not we who do the changing, but the Holy Spirit changes us from within. Therefore, our role is to seek Him with all our heart, mind, and strength, and He "who began a good work in you will carry it out to completion" (Phil 1:6).

Real change does not start with behavior change, but heart change. Simply changing behaviors is like tying on fresh apples to a dying apple tree. It might look good for a short time, but eventually these apples will die as well. In order to have good fruit growing from the tree, you need to take care of it at the root level. If you've ever tried to change and it was short lived, chances are the change was a fruit change, and not a root change. A root change requires a commitment to (1) cultivate the surrounding soil, (2) remove any hazards, and (3) add nutrients and water to the surrounding soil. In time, the roots will absorb what is necessary for the tree, and its fruit will be pleasing to the owner.

Cultivating the Soil

In the parable of the sower (Matt 13), Jesus explained the types of soil a sower spread his seeds on—the path, the rocky ground, the thorny ground, and the good soil. Each of these areas, except the good soil, had issues which prevented the Word of God from flourishing. The good soil represents the one who hears the Word, understands it and puts it into practice. Good soil produces a good tree with good roots and good fruit.

The necessary soil for a healthy tree includes soil that is not hard or compacted but allows water and air to penetrate it. This lets the roots receive water and nutrients to keep it healthy. Hard soil will prevent a healthy tree. Similarly, a hard heart will prevent the living water, the Holy Spirit, from supplying the believer with the spiritual necessities important for growth. Hardness of heart always includes pride and self-centeredness. Our pride presents itself in many ways. My way. I'm right—you're wrong. My needs over yours. When it's all about me, there is little to no room for God or anyone else unless they exist for my purposes.

If pride and self-centeredness are present in hardened soil, then it is logical that a heart of humility is essential for good soil. The first step to cultivating a hardened heart is to confess a prideful heart and seek forgiveness (Ps 51:17). Unless you are broken over your own pride and selfishness, the Spirit is not likely or willing to produce much fruit in you.

My favorite chapter and verses on humility are Philippians 2:1–11. Paul states, "Do nothing out of selfish ambition or vain conceit. Rather, in humility value others above yourselves, not looking to your own interests but each of you to the interests of the others" (3–4). Humility has everything to do with valuing others above ourselves. In our pride, we value ourselves above others. If we do value others, it is for what they can do for us instead of for who they are. In humility, we value others as though we are their servants looking to their interests. Instead of dismissing their thoughts, ideas, or feelings, we value them by responding with kind and loving words or actions. Instead of assuming the motives of others and telling them why they did things, we remain humble in our interpretations and choose to believe their reasons instead of our own. In doing so, we demonstrate that we love them, accept them and value who they are and not simply what they do. Instead of responding in accusatory tones or harsh words, we respond in gentle tones and words. When the soil of humility is cultivated, the fruits become beautiful in appearance, enticing for the observer, and pleasing to the King.

Humility is also necessary to become more like Christ. Continuing in Philippians 2:5–8, Paul writes:

In your relationships with one another, have the same mindset as Christ Jesus: Who, being in very nature God, did not consider equality with God something to be used to his own advantage; rather, he made himself nothing by taking the very nature of a servant, being made in human likeness. And being found in appearance as a man, he humbled himself by becoming obedient to death—even death on a cross!

Humility is the mindset, heart posture, and nature of Christ. While eternal and majestic, He became a finite and fragile human being. He even went one step lower and made Himself a servant, meeting the spiritual, emotional, and physical needs of those with whom He came into contact. His humility was seen in his treatment of others. His kindness, compassion, and love for sinners was evident to all He met. Jesus maintained a daily dependence toward God and prioritized time with Him, seeking direction and strength (Mk 1:35; Jn 11:41–42, 12:28 17; Luke 3:21, 5:16, 6:12, 9:18, 9:29, 11:1).

Jesus's humility was evident in His complete obedience to God the Father. He was even "obedient to death—even death on the cross." Obedience—following the complete will of God the Father—is the ultimate example of humility. Setting aside His own desires, Jesus was willing to suffer and place Himself in the hands of the Jews and Romans, willing to go through extreme torture because of His love for the Father and us. Obedience to God involves personal sacrifice, sometimes even our very lives. The sacrifices we make demonstrate that the One we obey has authority over our lives and actions. Obedience to God is our exercise in humility. But how?

Removing Hazards

Some of the greatest hazards a tree faces include exposed roots and diseases. Exposed roots are susceptible to wounds caused by lawnmowers or other machinery or tools. Open wounds in a tree, like in humans, can cause an infection which leaves the tree susceptible to rot or diseases that cause sicknesses and death. In our lives, wounds from the past or present may have a greater impact than we expect. Some of these wounds leave infections of bitterness, fear of intimacy, insecurities, and severe black-and-white thinking that harm relationships. Healing from these wounds can be a daunting process which may require the help of a trained, Christ-centered counselor.

Scripture teaches us to remove the hazards in our lives by putting off the old and putting on the new. Consider Paul's statement in Ephesians 4: "You were taught, with regard to your former way of life, to put off your old self, which is being corrupted by its deceitful desires to be made new in the attitude of your minds; and to put on the new self, created to be like God in true righteousness and holiness" (22–24). Putting off the old self is not simply putting off bad behaviors, but about changing the "deceitful desires" within. In other words, it's a heart change. Putting off the old self will also be about putting off old patterns. Trying harder at doing the same thing will yield the same results. Trying something different and new will often yield different and new results. What are the old behavioral and heart issues we ought to put off?

We ought to remove some obvious behaviors: lying, cursing, name-calling, intimidation, threats of divorce or harm, manipulating, sexual demands and sins, gossip, addictions, envy. Getting rid of these behaviors is a step in the right direction, but falls short of genuine heart change. Real heart change will lead to our desires changing, overcoming fears and addictions, and reducing the frequency and intensity of our anger. The book *How People Change* by Paul Tripp and Timothy Lane is a great resource for learning how to personally change to become more like Christ.[6] If you've been accused of domestic abuse, I'd encourage you to read Chris Moles' book, *The Heart of Domestic Abuse.*[7]

Some less obvious hazardous behaviors to correct may include withdrawing from people when we are upset, ceasing our negative self-talk when we are upset with ourselves, and speaking about our feelings or concerns instead of internalizing them. Behaviors to remove include vocalizing our feelings and thoughts without a filter, controlling actions, being critical or complaining, etc. There are many sinful behaviors that are best to eradicate from our lives. We will not be perfect in this endeavor, by any means, because we will always struggle with our flesh. Even Paul admitted there was a battle within and he often lost, but he continued to turn to the Savior (Rom 7:15–25).

Putting off the old self is also about denying ourselves. Denying ourselves is not about letting people always get their way and being a doormat, but it is about saying no to our sinful wants, desires, and demands and yes to the Spirit. Jesus said, "Whoever wants to be my disciple must deny themselves and take up their cross and follow me." (Mt 16:24). Denying ourselves is essential to being a follower of Jesus because the old self is corrupted by our selfish hearts. We cannot follow Him if we follow our sinful hearts. We cannot follow both because they lead us in opposite directions—one toward life and the other toward death—death of relationships with God and others, and possibly even physical death.

Jake struggled to admit he was wrong. It was the subject of many fights between he and his wife. He admitted there was something inside of him that simply couldn't say, "I was wrong." Admitting that he was wrong and others were right was a blow to his pride. Understanding the need to put on humility, Jake began to accept being a sinner meant he was imperfect, which meant he would be wrong, choose wrong, and perceive things incorrectly at times. He began to understand that his standing before God stemmed from Christ's righteousness and perfection, and not his own. Therefore, Jake began to admit to others when he was wrong or perceived things incorrectly. He refused to defend himself, blame others, minimize his mistakes, or beat himself up, but he would accept responsibility for his actions. Jake saw himself as broken, but allowed Christ to define him, defend him, and deliver him from himself. When Jake turned to Christ, he felt a freedom inside of him that came through humility. When he was unsuccessful, he felt trapped in his pride and anger. While this was difficult for Jake, in time he began to see positive differences in his relationships at home, work, and church. Some people were making comments about his positive attitude, and he was experiencing less conflict at home. Jake was becoming more like Christ.

Adding Water and Nutrients

Cultivating the soil and removing hazards are the first two steps to heal a fruit-bearing tree. The third step is to add water and nutrients to the tree and its roots. Without water, nothing would survive on earth. This is why Jesus states that he is the fountain of living water (Jn 4:14, 7:38; Jer 17:13), and through faith in Christ we become fountains of living water (Jn 4:14, 7:37–39). We need His sustenance and the world needs believers to be mini fountains of God's grace.

In John 4, a Samaritan woman arrived at a well in the middle of the day to retrieve some water. Her timing at the well indicated she was shunned by many women who arrived at the well in the morning when the heat was bearable. It was likely she was someone who had loose morals, and later we learned she, at minimum, had struggles with men. Jesus approached the woman and after He asked for water, He offered her living water so she would never thirst again. After Jesus told her what He knew about her life, the woman spoke to others in the community and they came to believe in Jesus as the Savior of the world. The Samaritan woman had a need inside of her that she was trying to fill with men. In the end, it wasn't the love of men that could fill her emptiness, it was only the love of Jesus who could satisfy her greatest needs.

John the Baptist said, "He [Jesus] must increase, but I must decrease" (Jn 3:30). In other words, we need more of Jesus and less of ourselves. Black-and-white thinkers ought to pay close attention to Jesus in the Gospels, specifically how he related to people, like the woman at the well and the woman caught in adultery (Jn 8:1–11). While recognizing their sins, His treatment of them was based on their worth in God's eyes, not on their actions. Many black-and-white thinkers pay closer attention to Jesus's rebukes of the Pharisees and the disciples because they are drawn to truth and justice like most men are drawn to action movies with themes of justice or revenge. (We also like seeing things get blown up!).

Many are also drawn to Jesus in Revelation where he separates the wheat from the chaff, judges the earth, and rules the new heaven and earth. Jesus as judge or conqueror is extremely important for us to understand, but the Jesus black-and-white thinkers need to focus on more is Jesus as the grace-giver. Grace-giving Jesus values the person over performance, empathy over expectations, and spiritual needs over somatic wants. While still addressing wrongs gently, Jesus prioritized people and relationships.

In His offer of living water, Jesus offers Himself to us. His desire is to sustain us daily and give us all we need to produce the fruit that keeps with repentance (Mt 3:8) and live a transformed life for Him. What does this fruit look like? Paul writes about it! It is "love, joy, peace, patience, kindness, goodness, faithfulness, gentleness, and self-control" (Gal 5:22–23). Ask yourself, do my life and relationships reflect the fruit that comes from the Spirit, or the fruit that comes from my own damaged soil and tree?

Our goal is not to do more, but to surrender to the One who is doing more in us. It's denying the desires of our flesh (Luke 9:23) and agreeing with the Holy Spirit's work in us to conform us to the likeness of Christ (Rom 8:29).

We need to remind ourselves daily that God's not done. He began a good work in you and He will not simply stop, but continue to work in you and through you until you are with Him in heaven or until Christ returns (Phil 1:6). Either way, this means there is hope for change.

Cultivate your soil in humility. Remove the diseases of sin through brokenness and confession, and allow Christ to reign in you to produce the fruit of His Spirit. This change does not happen overnight; it is a process. I have, however, seen the process go by quicker for those who have been completely broken over their sins and the impact those sins had on another. The process goes much slower for people who are focused on their own hurts and the other person's sins. Dwelling on our own suffering and being the victim of the other person's sins will hinder change. True brokenness over sin starts with recognizing that we are the offender. Relational reconciliation continues with understanding how our sins affected the other person. While our hurts are important, we are in a better place of dealing with them after we first remove the logs in our own eyes, because only then can we see more clearly (Matt 7:5).

Reflection Questions

1. Have you ever tried to change by yourself and without the help of Christ? How long did this change last?

2. If you were to take a spiritual heart test, would your heart reflect a hardened, embittered and self-centered heart, or a heart that is humble and ready to be cultivated by the Spirit?

3. What are some obvious hazards in your life that are preventing your roots from growing? Are there past wounds which need to be healed, people who need to be forgiven, insecurities that need to be addressed, behaviors that need to be removed? Make an action plan to address these issues.

4. How will you add more of Christ to your life? Prayer? Study? Attending church more? What do you need to deny in yourself to make more room for Christ? Activities? Sin?

Final Words

Black-and-white thinkers are created in the image of God. Their interpretive lens reflects His moral traits, as expressed throughout the Old Testament. Black-and-white thinkers perceive situations through standards, give credence to processes, procedures and structure, and have an all-or-nothing approach to much of life. Although some black-and-white thinkers apply such thinking in every aspect of their lives, many black-and-white thinkers are more relational and, as a result, enjoy better relationships. Those who think almost exclusively in black and white often struggle in relationships and may become abusive emotionally or physically if pride, self-centeredness and insecurity reign.

The black-and-white thinkers' strengths include their ability to see things logically, plan accordingly, and to work well in concrete subjects. They are often reliable and hard workers who either pick up the slack of underperformers or hold them accountable to a standard. Many black-and-white thinkers struggle with abstractions: philosophy, emotions, and relationships. They can overcome their weaknesses in humility by working together, making friends with or marrying someone whose strengths match their weaknesses. The more one recognizes their own strengths and weaknesses as well as the other's, the easier it is to relate and work together.

The black-and-white thinking Christian can learn from the example of Saul-turned-Paul in the New Testament. After his Damascus Road experience, through the power of the Holy Spirit, Paul humbled himself and applied grace to his life and demonstrated this grace to others. Paul allowed God to transform him into a more Christ-like person. As a result, Paul became more effective for the kingdom of God. While he continued to acknowledge standards, he lived by grace, preached grace, and extended grace to those he ministered to, and in doing so, reflected Christ more fully. When we recognize our need for change, and humbly decide to partner with the Holy Spirit's work, He will begin to transform us to be more effective in ministry, in relationships, and in life.

I trust this book has been helpful to you in your personal journey in growing to become more like Christ. I hope it has been one of the many Christ-centered resources that assists you in your desire to become better in relationships, or if you're not a black-and-white thinker, helps you to better understand the black-and-white thinking Christian. May the Lord continue to guide you in your life, relationships, and faith.

May the grace of the Lord Jesus Christ, and the love of God, and the fellowship of the Holy Spirit be with you all.
—2 Cor 13:14

Appendix A

The Black-and-White Thinking Quiz

Answer each question by placing a Y or N next to the corresponding number. Count the number of Y's to determine the level of black-and-white thinking you may possess.

1. Do you tend to see things as all good or all bad?
2. Do you find yourself focused on one thing and ignore everything else?
3. Do you see yourself as either a success or a failure?
4. Do you cut yourself off from relationships?
5. Do you cut others off from a relationship with you?
6. Do you struggle with compassion and empathy?
7. Do you judge others or their actions according to standards?
8. Are you a perfectionist?
9. Do you think people should meet standards or expectations?
10. Do you argue with others about what is right versus wrong?
11. Are you "all in" or "all out" with activities?
12. Do you speak in absolute terms, such as always-never, either-or in conversations?
13. Do you struggle to understand others' emotions?
14. Do you prefer people get to the point instead of "beating around the bush"?
15. Do you work well with things that are more concrete, such as facts, figures, processes and procedures?

Count the number of Y's to determine the level of black-and-white thinking you may possess.

Appendix A

1–5 Y's = Some Black-and-White thinking
6–10 Y's = Moderate Black-and-White Thinking
11–15 Y's = More Severe in Black-and-White Thinking

0 – No Black-and-White Thinking

This quiz did not pick up on any black-and-white thinking, but that does not mean it is not present in any area of your life. Pay attention to areas where you may have tendencies toward perfectionism or higher expectations for yourself or others and challenge these areas with God's grace. You are likely a relational thinker who is more in touch with your own emotions and the emotions of those around you. You are likely compassionate and empathetic, but this may lead you to make decisions that may not be in your best interest (i.e. lack of boundaries, saying yes to others, enabling, etc.).

1–5 – Some Black-and-White Thinking

There are some areas in your life where you tend to possess black-and-white thinking, but you are probably not a black-and-white thinker. You may be more of a relational thinker, or possess a good amount of relational thinking. You also may find yourself in close relationships with either relational thinkers or black-and-white thinkers.

6–10 – Moderate Black-and-White Thinking

You are most likely a black-and-white thinker. There are areas in your life where you think in black-in-white and would do well to grow in humility and grace. You are likely to have positive relationships with others, mixing relational skills with your black-and-white thinking, but can be insensitive to the emotions of those around you. Be mindful as

141

Appendix A

to which areas in your life you think in black-and-white and challenge
yourself to expand your thinking according to God's love and grace.

11–15 – Severe Black-and-White Thinking

You are a black-and-white thinker. You are admired for your strengths,
yet your strengths are also your relational weaknesses. You likely avoid
feeling your own emotions and are prone to overlook others' emotions
as well. Your busyness and attention to detail are admired by
employers, but cause problems in relationships. If you are married to a
relational thinker, listen to their feedback on relationships with others.
If you allow pride and insecurity to reign in your life, you may become
narcissistic or emotionally abusive. Try not to react to others but
respond by speaking truth only when it is in love. Or do not speak at
all. Continue to work on grace and humility in your life and seek help
in your struggle with relationships. Make sure you address any pride
and insecurity in your life through the gospel of grace and love as
demonstrated through Christ.

NOTES

1. "Defining Maturity," Article, accessed March 30, 2019, *www.paultripp.com/articles/posts/defining-maturity*

2. Tim S. Lane and Paul Tripp, *Relationship: A Mess Worth Making* (Greensboro, NC: New Growth Press, 2006), 36.

3. Nancy Leigh DeMoss, *Broken: The Heart God Revives*, (Chicago: Moody Publishers, 2005), 88-100. Used by permission.

4. "Depression," Mayo Clinic, accessed March 30, 2019, *www.mayoclinic.org/diseases-conditions/depression/symptomps-causes/syc-20356007.*

5. "Mental Health Conditions," National Alliance on Mental Illness, accessed February 15, 2019, *https://www.nami.org/learn-more/mental-health-conditions.*

6. Tim S. Lane and Paul Tripp, *How People Change* (Greensboro, NC: New Growth Press, 2008).

7. Chris Moles, *The Heart of Domestic Abuse* (Bemidji, MN: Focus Publishing, 2015).

8. Edward Welch, *Depression: A Stubborn Darkness,* (Greensboro, NC: New Growth Press, 2011).

Other Resources by Fred Jacoby, MA

Blog: *https://foundchristcounsel.wordpress.com*

King of the Road: Overcoming Road Rage
(Booklet)

COMING SOON…

Tentatively titled…

By Design

Created Like Him. Relating Like Him.

Becoming Like Him.

Subscribe for updates at:

www.fredjacoby.com

facebook.com/fredkjacoby

Made in the USA
Coppell, TX
26 May 2020

26466783R00085